For Engineers & Designers

KOMPAS-3D EXERCISES

200 3D PRACTICE DRAWINGS

SACHIDANAND JHA

Dear Reader,

Thank you for choosing **KOMPAS-3D Exercises** book. This book is part of a family of premium-quality CADIN360 books, all of which are written by Outstanding author who combine practical experience with a gift for teaching.

CADIN360 was founded in 2016. More than 3 years later, we're still committed to producing consistently exceptional books. With each of our titles, we're working hard to set a new standard for the industry. From the paper we print on, to the authors we work with, our goal is to bring you the best books available.

I hope you see all that reflected in these pages. I'd be very interested to hear your comments and get your feedback on how we're doing. Feel free to let me know what you think about this or any other CADIN360 book by sending me an email at contactus@cadin360.com.

If you think you've found a technical error in this book, please visit https://cadin360.com/contact-us/.
Customer feedback is critical to our efforts at CADIN360.

Best regards,

Sachidanand Jha
Founder & CEO, CADIN360

KOMPAS-3D Exercises

Published by
CADIN360
cadin360.com
Copyright © 2019 by CADIN360, All rights reserved.

Limit of Liability/Disclaimer of Warranty:

Examination Copies

Electronic Files

Disclaimer:

Preface

KOMPAS-3D Exercises

❖ This book contain 200 CAD practice exercises and drawings.

❖ This book does not provide step by step tutorial to design 3D models.

❖ S.I Unit is used.

❖ Predominantly used Third Angle Projection.

❖ This book is for **KOMPAS-3D** and Other Feature-Based Modeling Software such as Inventor, SolidWorks, NX, Solid Edge, AutoCAD, PTC Creo etc.

❖ It is intended to provide Drafters, Designers and Engineers with enough 3D CAD exercises for practice on **KOMPAS-3D**.

❖ It includes almost all types of exercises that are necessary to provide, clear, concise and systematic information required on industrial machine part drawings.

❖ Third Angle Projection is intentionally used to familiarize Drafters, Designers and Engineers in Third Angle Projection to meet the expectation of world wide Engineering drawing print.

❖ Clear and well drafted drawing help easy understanding of the design.

❖ This book is for Beginner, Intermediate and Advance CAD users.

❖ These exercises are from Basics to Advance level.

❖ Each exercises can be assigned and designed separately.

❖ No Exercise is a prerequisite for another. All dimensions are in mm.

❖ Note: Assume any missing dimensions.

EX-01

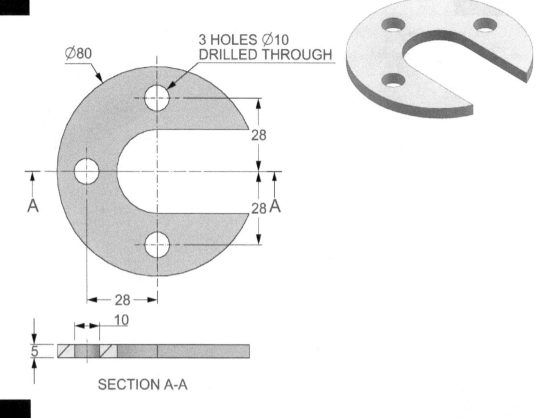

Ø80

3 HOLES Ø10
DRILLED THROUGH

28

28 A

A

28

10

5

SECTION A-A

EX-02

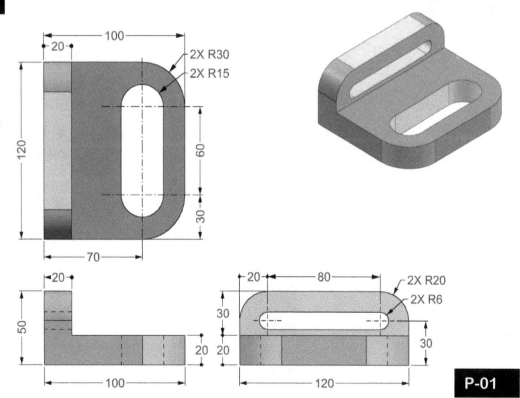

100

20

2X R30

2X R15

120

60

30

70

20

50

20

100

20

80

2X R20

2X R6

30

20 20

30

120

P-01

EX-03

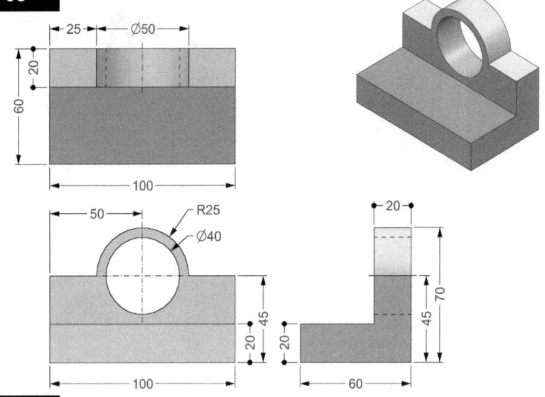

25   Ø50

20

60

100

50   R25   Ø40

45   100   20   20

20   60   45   70

EX-04

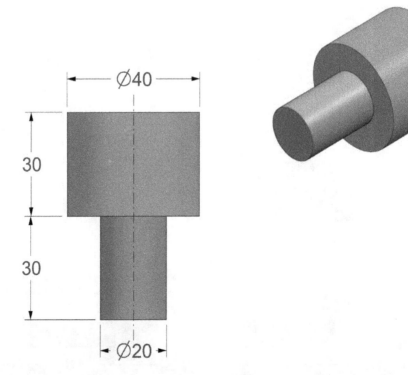

Ø40

30

30

Ø20

P-02

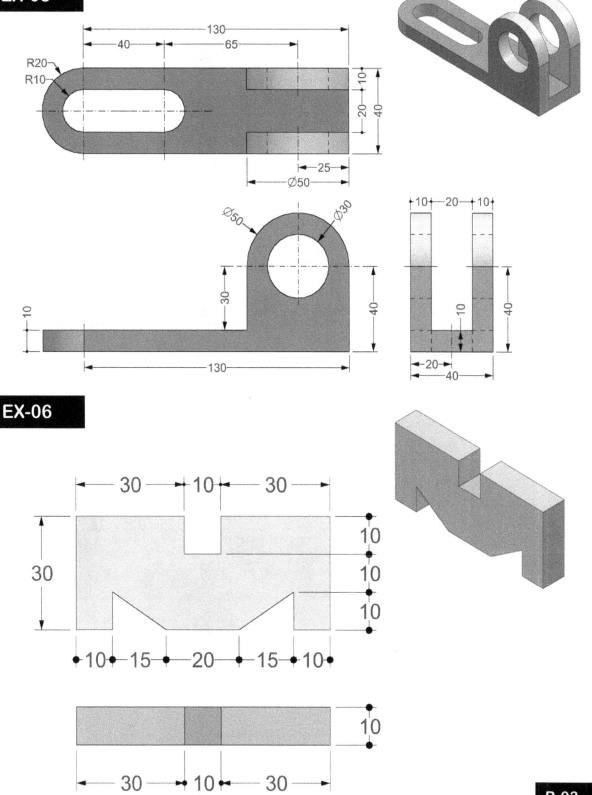

EX-05

EX-06

P-03

EX-07

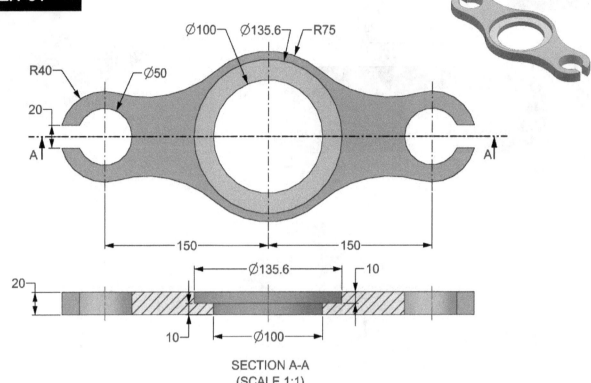

Ø100 Ø135.6 R75

R40 Ø50

20

A A

150 150

SECTION A-A
(SCALE 1:1)

Ø135.6 10

20

10 Ø100

EX-08

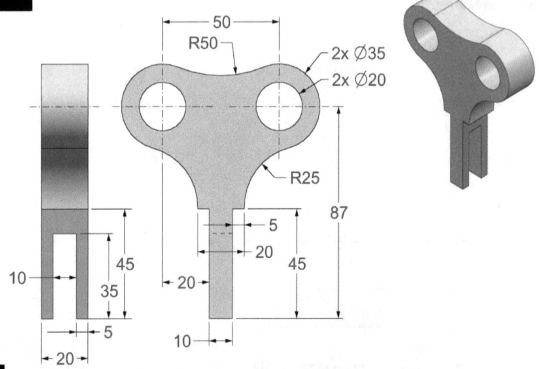

50

R50

2x Ø35

2x Ø20

R25

87

5

20

45

45

10

10

35

5

20

20

10

P-04

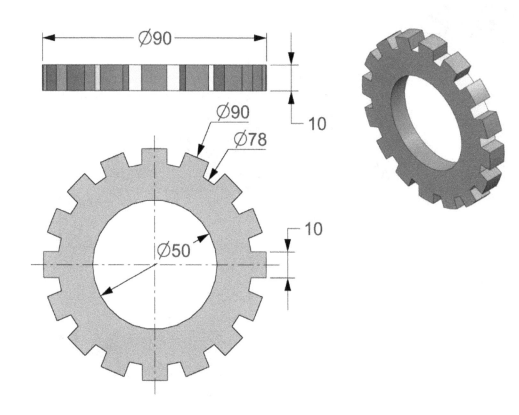

⌀90

10

⌀90
⌀78

10

⌀50

R15
⌀15
⌀20
40
50
⌀12
40
⌀30
A
40
R50
A
⌀40
R30
85

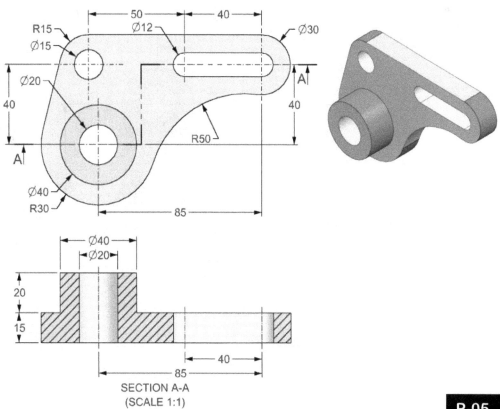

⌀40
⌀20
20
15
40
85

SECTION A-A
(SCALE 1:1)

EX-11

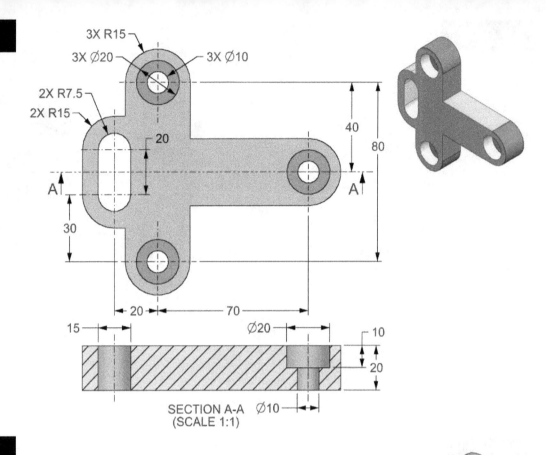

3X R15
3X ⌀20
3X ⌀10
2X R7.5
2X R15
20
40
80
A
A
30
20
70
15
⌀20
10
20
⌀10

SECTION A-A
(SCALE 1:1)

EX-12

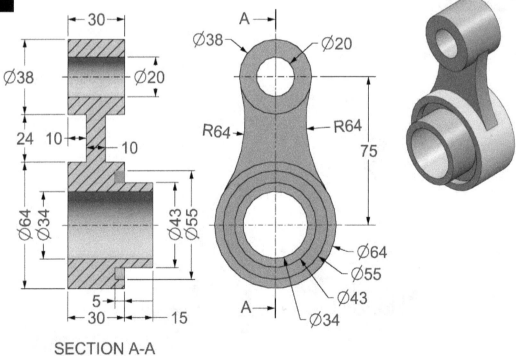

30
⌀38
⌀20
24
10
10
⌀64
⌀34
⌀43
⌀55
5
30
15

A
⌀38
⌀20
R64
R64
75
⌀64
⌀55
⌀43
⌀34
A

SECTION A-A
(SCALE 1:1)

P-06

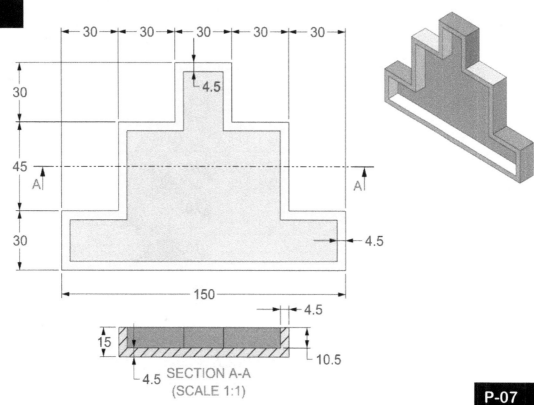

EX-13

10 | 50
10 | 30

5

40 20

40 30 20

R10

15

2X R5
2X Ø10

20 | 30
70

EX-14

30 | 30 | 30 | 30 | 30

30

4.5

45

A | A

30

4.5

150

4.5

15

10.5

4.5 SECTION A-A
(SCALE 1:1)

P-07

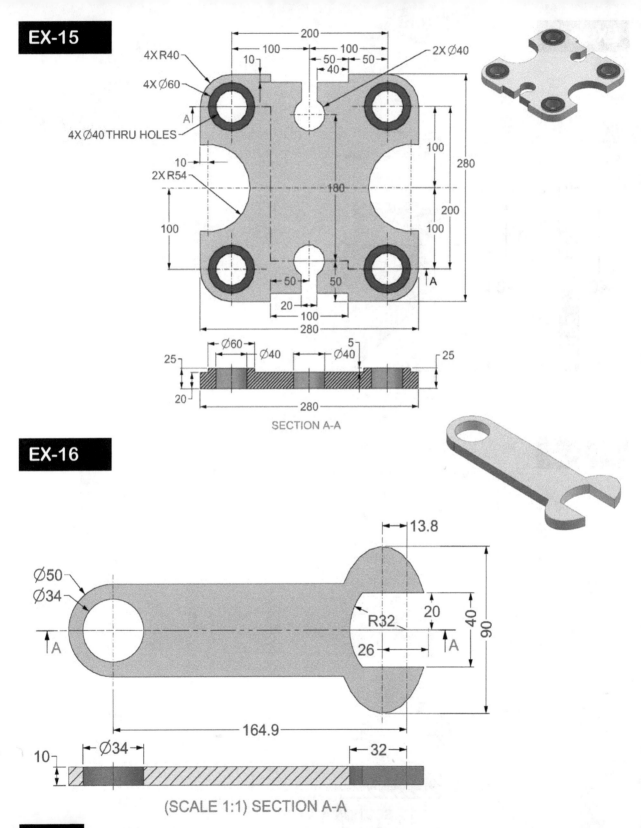

EX-15

4X R40
4X Ø60
4X Ø40 THRU HOLES
2X R54

200
100
100
10
50
50
40
2X Ø40

A

100
280
180
200
100

10

100

50
50
20
100
280

Ø60
Ø40
5
Ø40

25
25
25
20
280

SECTION A-A

EX-16

13.8

Ø50
Ø34

R32
20
40
90
26

A
A

164.9

10
Ø34
32

(SCALE 1:1) SECTION A-A

P-08

EX-17

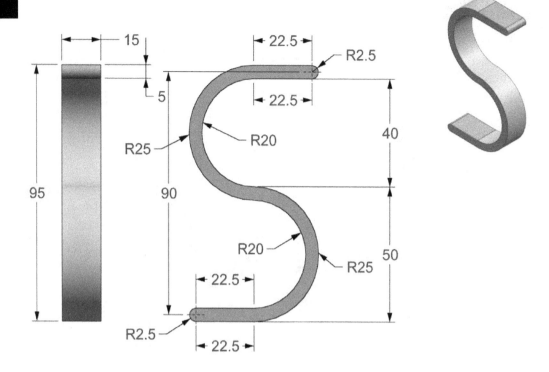

EX-18

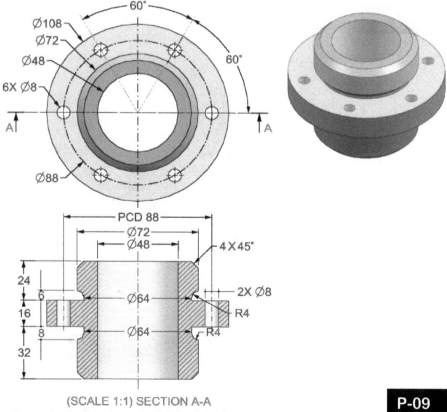

(SCALE 1:1) SECTION A-A

P-09

EX-19

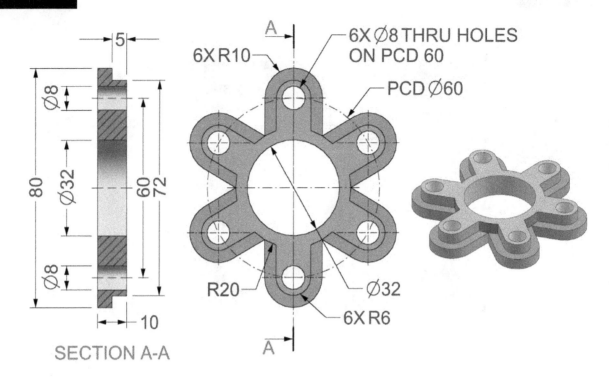

6X R10

6X Ø8 THRU HOLES
ON PCD 60

PCD Ø60

Ø8

Ø32

60

72

80

Ø8

10

5

SECTION A-A

A

A

R20

6X R6

Ø32

EX-20

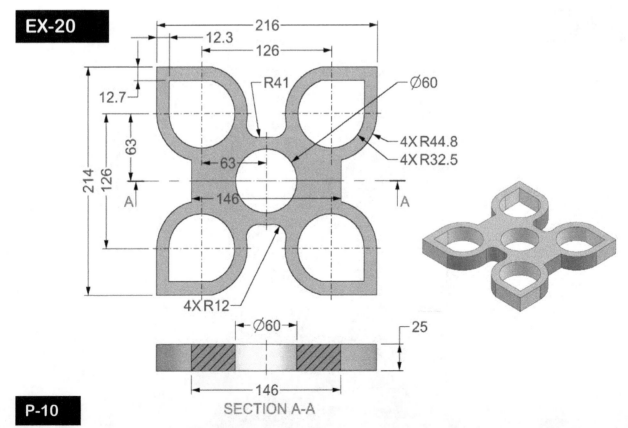

216

12.3

126

12.7

R41

Ø60

63

214

126

63

4X R44.8

4X R32.5

146

A

A

4X R12

Ø60

25

146

SECTION A-A

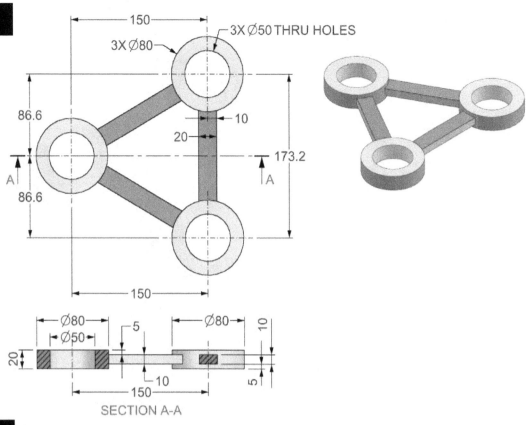

3X Ø50 THRU HOLES
3X Ø80
150
86.6
86.6
10
20
173.2
A
A
150

SECTION A-A
Ø80
Ø50
20
5
10
150
Ø80
10
5

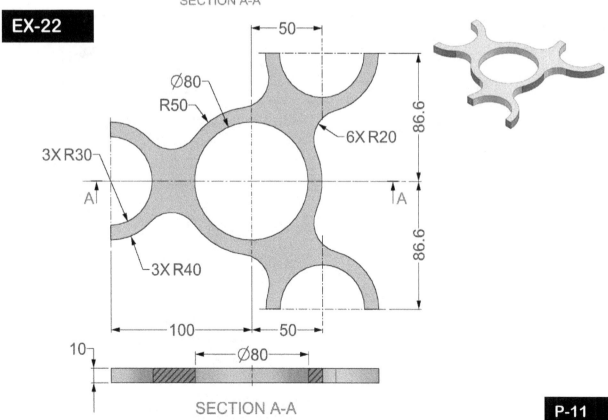

50
Ø80
R50
86.6
6X R20
3X R30
A
A
3X R40
86.6
100
50
10
Ø80

SECTION A-A

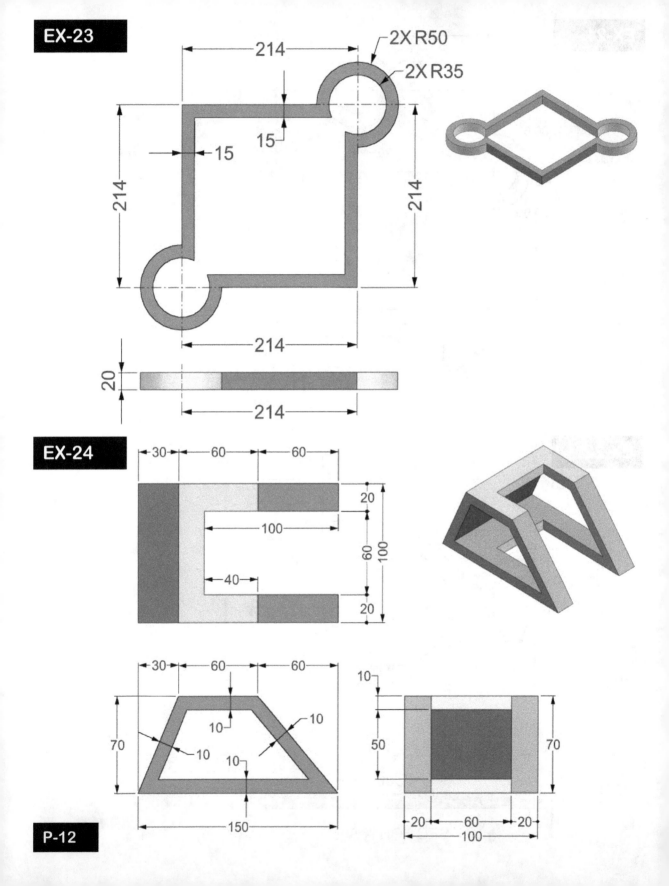

EX-23

214

2X R50

2X R35

15

15

214

214

214

214

20

214

EX-24

30 · 60 · 60

20

100

60

100

40

20

30 · 60 · 60

10

10

10

70

10

10

150

10

50

70

20 · 60 · 20

100

P-12

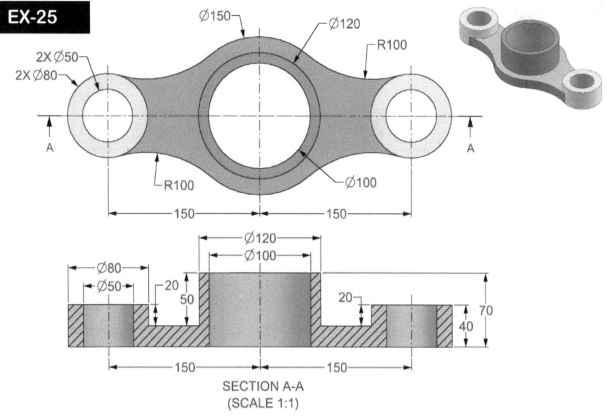

Ø150
Ø120
R100
2X Ø50
2X Ø80
R100
Ø100
150
150

Ø80
Ø50
20
50
Ø120
Ø100
20
70
40
150
150

SECTION A-A
(SCALE 1:1)

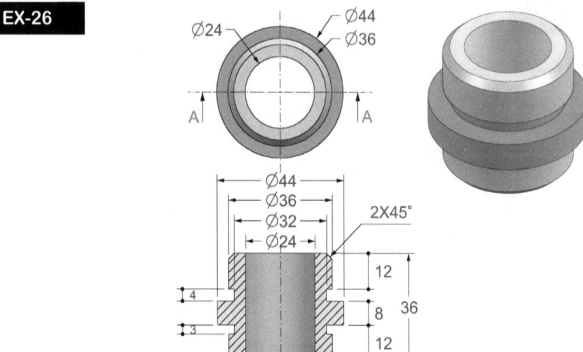

Ø24
Ø44
Ø36

A   A

Ø44
Ø36
Ø32
Ø24
2X45°
12
4
8   36
3
12

SECTION A-A
(SCALE 1:1)

EX-27

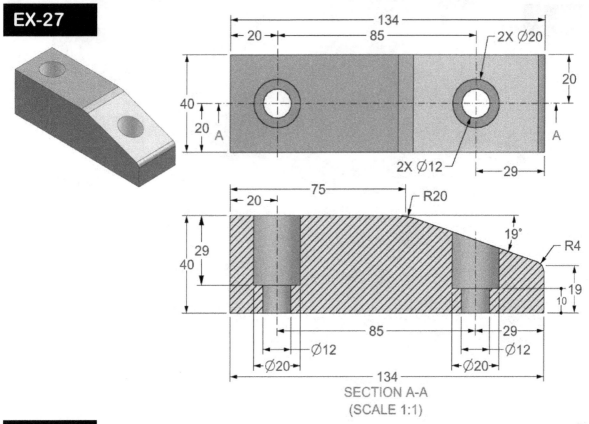

134
20
85
2X Ø20
20
40
20
A
A
2X Ø12
29

20
75
R20
19°
R4
29
40
19
10
85
29
Ø12
Ø12
Ø20
Ø20
134
SECTION A-A
(SCALE 1:1)

EX-28

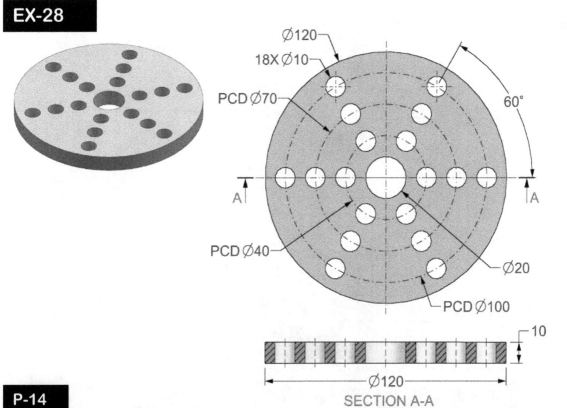

Ø120
18X Ø10
PCD Ø70
60°
PCD Ø40
Ø20
PCD Ø100
A
A

10
Ø120
SECTION A-A

EX-29

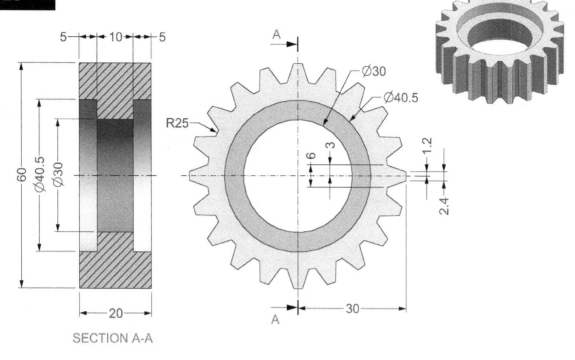

SECTION A-A

EX-30

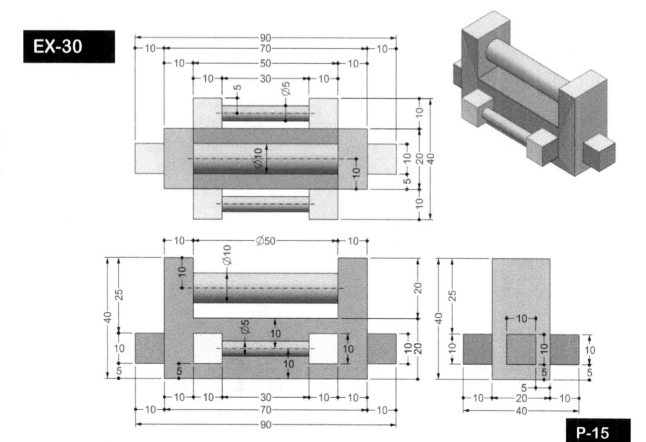

P-15

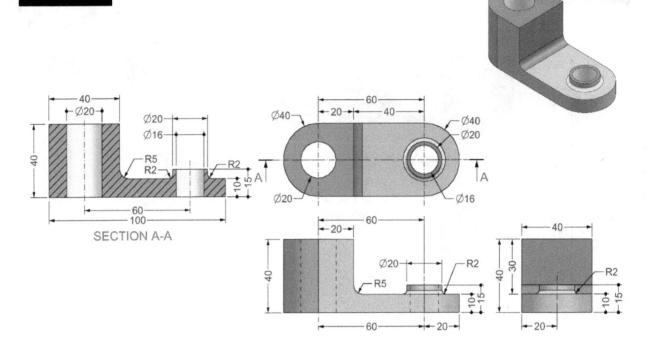

SECTION A-A

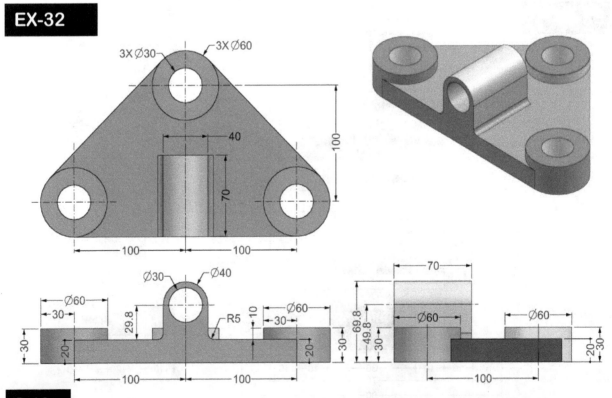

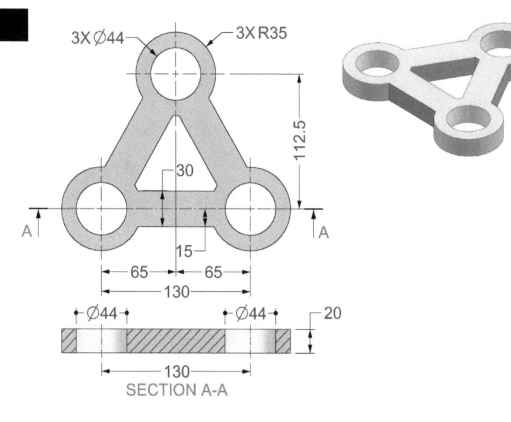

3X Ø44 — 3X R35

112.5

30

15

65 — 65

130

Ø44 — Ø44 — 20

130

SECTION A-A

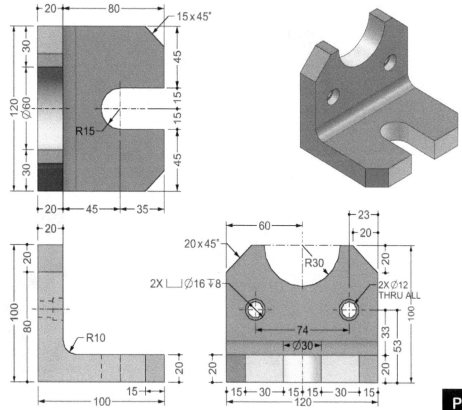

20 — 80 — 15 x 45°

30

45

120

Ø60

15 15

15

R15

30

45

20 — 45 — 35

20

20

100

80

R10

100

15

20 — 60 — 23

20 x 45° — 20

R30

2X ⌴ Ø16 ↧8 — 2X Ø12 THRU ALL

20

74

100

33

53

Ø30

20

20

15 — 30 — 15 15 — 30 — 15

120

EX-35

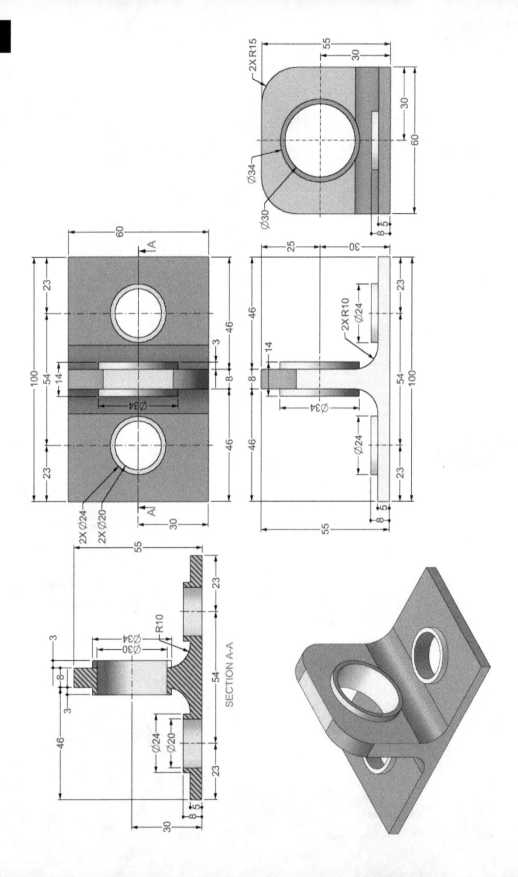

2X R15
55
30
30
60
Ø34
Ø30
8
5

60
A
23
46
100
54
14
3
8
Ø34
46
23
30
A
2X Ø24
2X Ø20

25
30
46
14
8
2X R10
Ø24
23
54
100
Ø34
Ø24
46
23
8
5
55

55
23
3
Ø34
Ø30
R10
8
54
3
46
Ø24
Ø20
23
8
5
30

SECTION A-A

P-18

EX-36

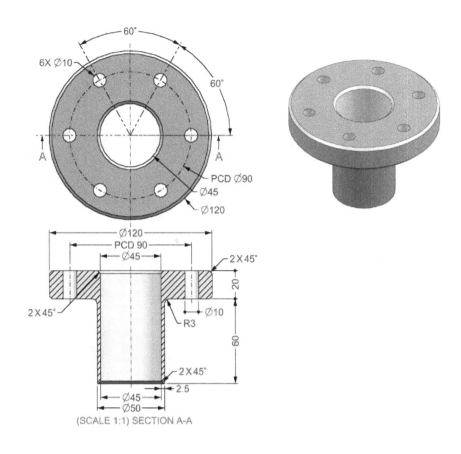

60°
60°
6X Ø10
PCD Ø90
Ø45
Ø120

A — A

Ø120
PCD 90
Ø45
2 X 45°
2 X 45°
Ø10
R3
20
60
2 X 45°
2.5
Ø45
Ø50

(SCALE 1:1) SECTION A-A

EX-37

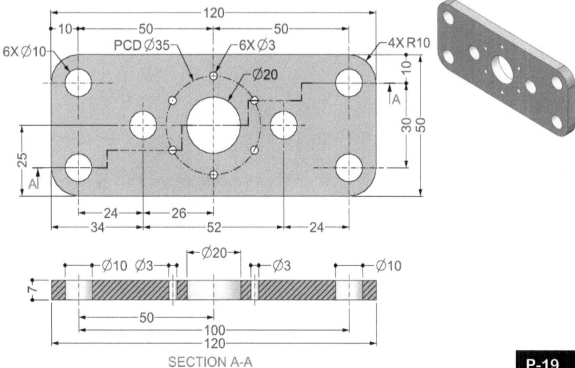

120
10
50
50
PCD Ø35
6X Ø3
4X R10
6X Ø10
Ø20
10
A
30
50
25
A
24
26
34
52
24

Ø10   Ø3
Ø20
Ø3
Ø10
7
50
100
120

SECTION A-A

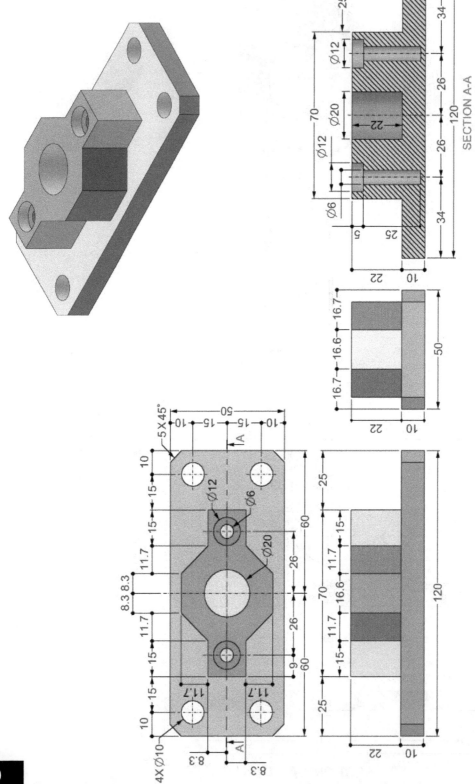

SECTION A-A

Ø12
Ø20
22
Ø12
Ø6

25
34
26
120
26
34

70

5
25
22
10

16.7 16.6 16.7
16.7 16.6 16.7
50
22
10

5 X 45°
50
10 15 15 10
A

Ø12
Ø6
Ø20

10
15
15
11.7
8.3 8.3
11.7
15
15
10
11.7 11.7

60
26
26
9
60

8.3
8.3
A

4X Ø10

25
15
11.7
70
16.6
11.7
15
25

120

22
10

EX-39

70

R20
Ø20

40

45

R25
Ø20

45

20

30

10

A

A

10

45

65

20

2X R10

Ø40

Ø20

25

45

SECTION A-A

EX-40

Ø60

20

10

5

Ø50

Ø60
Ø50

5 10 5

30

Ø60

20

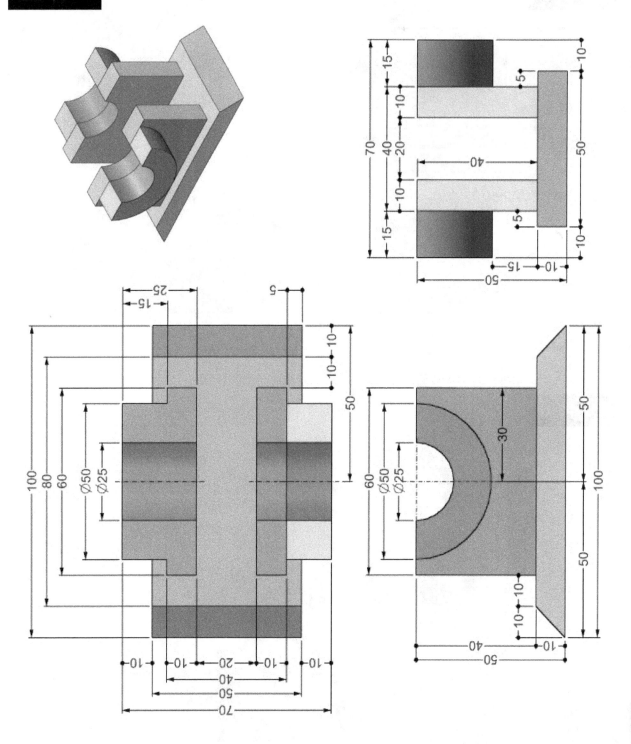

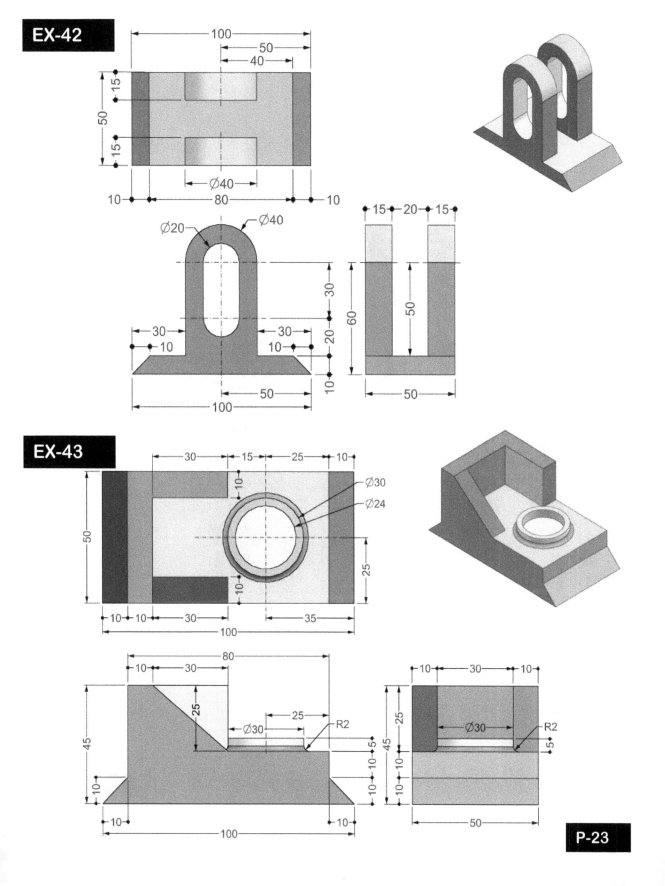

EX-42

EX-43

P-23

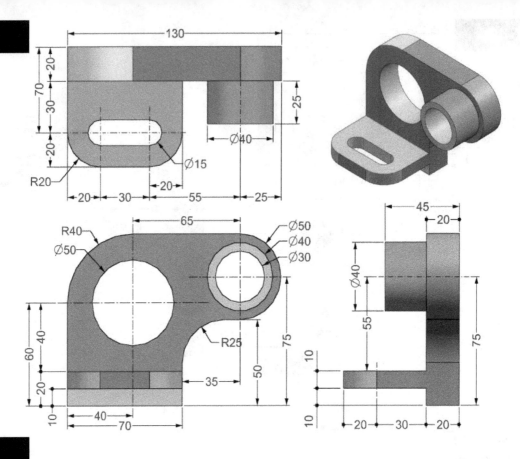

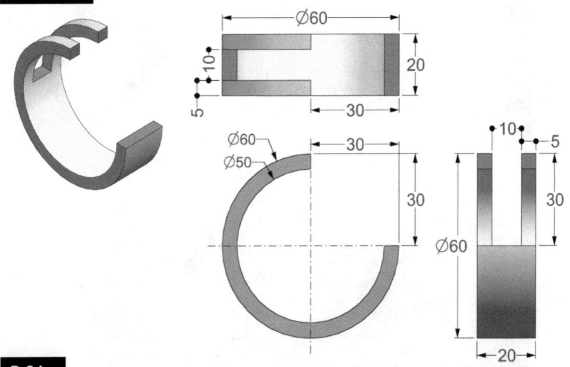

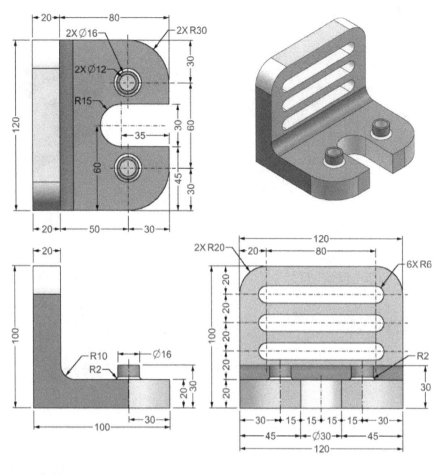

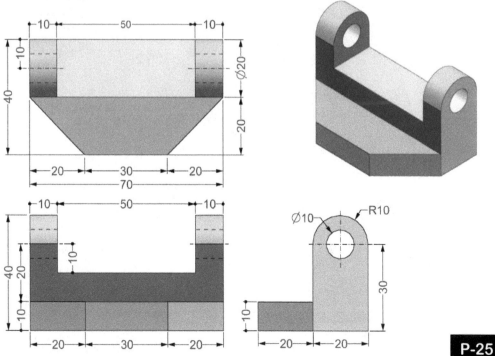

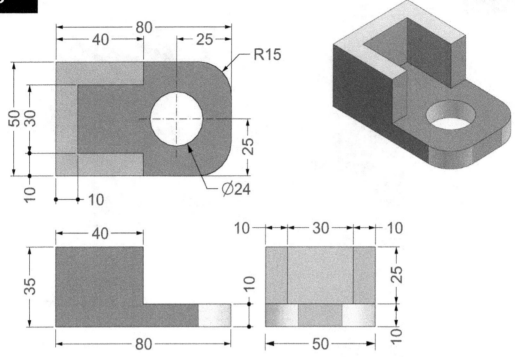

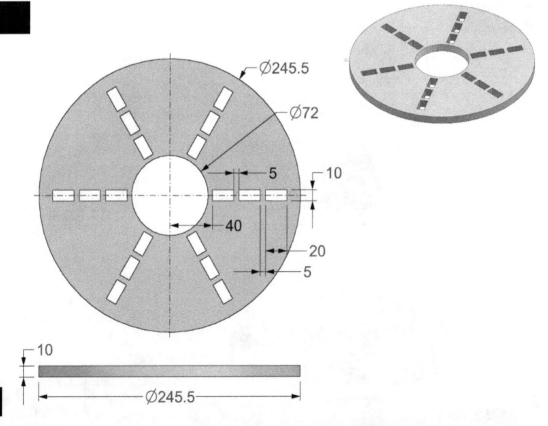

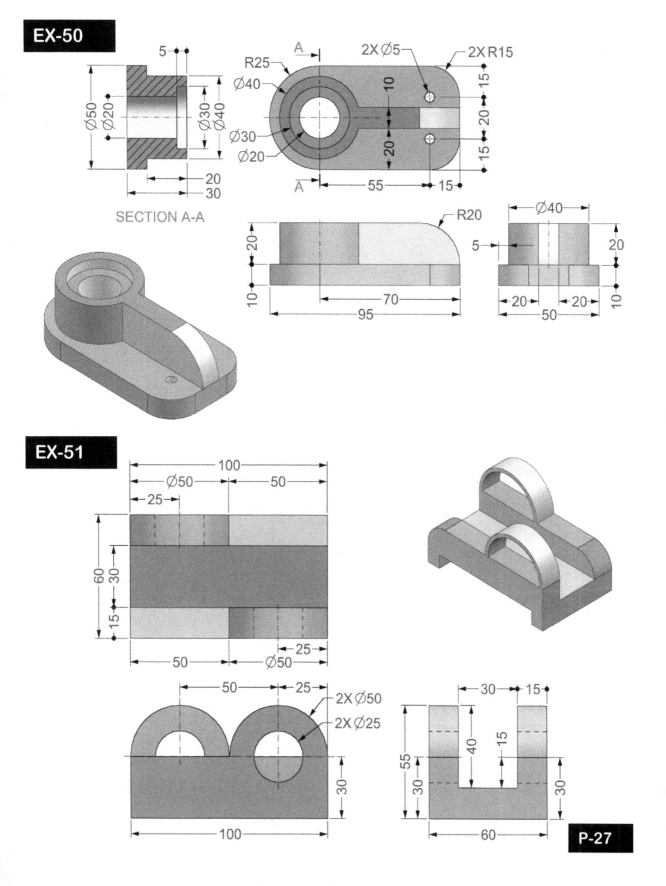

EX-50

R25
Ø40
Ø30
Ø20

2X Ø5
2X R15

10
20
20

15
20
15

55
15

SECTION A-A

Ø50
Ø20
Ø30
Ø40

5
20
30

R20
20
10
70
95

Ø40
5
20
20
20
50
10

EX-51

100
Ø50
50
25
60
30
15
50
Ø50
25

50
25
2X Ø50
2X Ø25
30
100

30
15
55
30
40
15
30
60

P-27

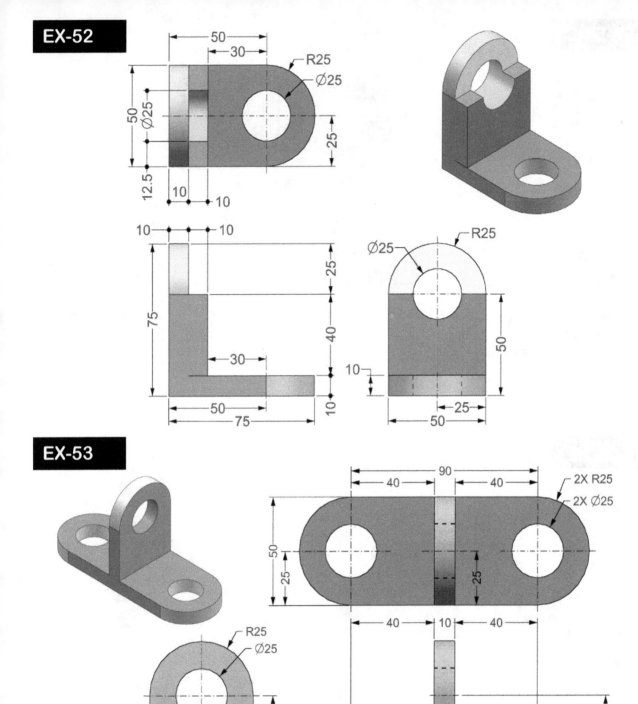

EX-52

EX-53

P-28

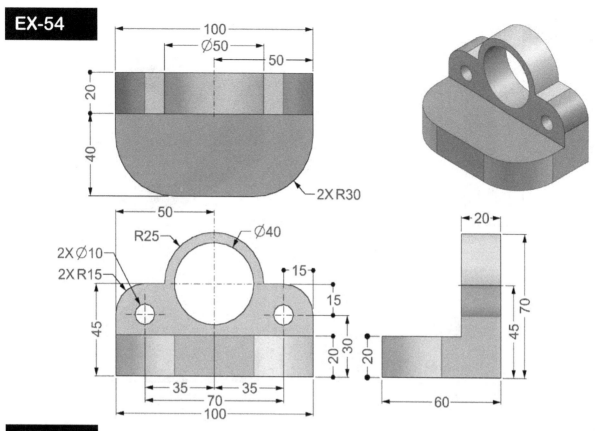

2X R30

100
Ø50
50
20
40

50
R25
Ø40
2X Ø10
2X R15
15
15
45
20
30
35
35
70
100

20
70
45
20
60

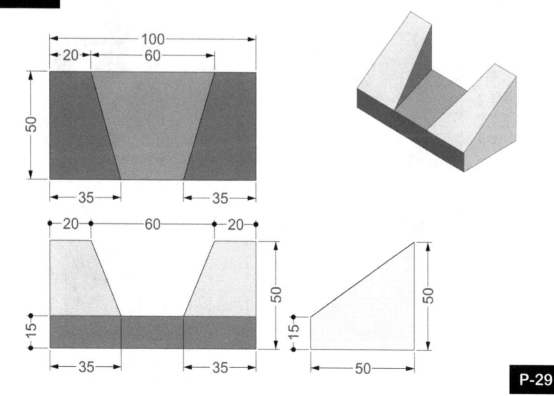

100
20
60
50
35
35

20
60
20
50
15
35
35

50
15
50

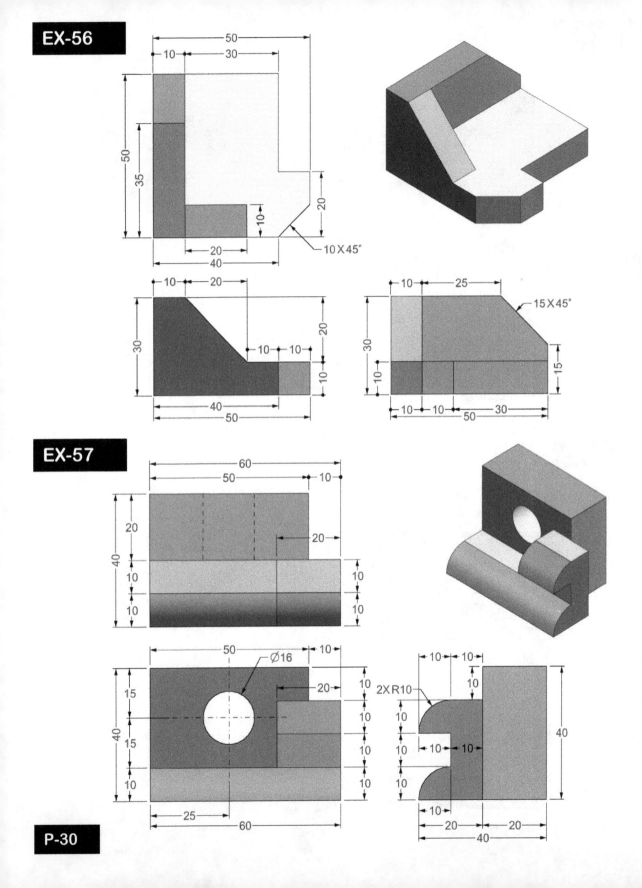

EX-56

50
10
30
50
35
50
20
10
20
40
10 X 45°

10
20
30
20
10
10
10
40
50

10
25
15 X 45°
30
10
15
10
10
50
30

EX-57

60
50
10
20
40
20
10
20
10
10
10

50
Ø16
10
20
10
15
10
2X R10
10
10
40
15
10
10
10
10
10
10
10
10
10
25
60
20
20
40

P-30

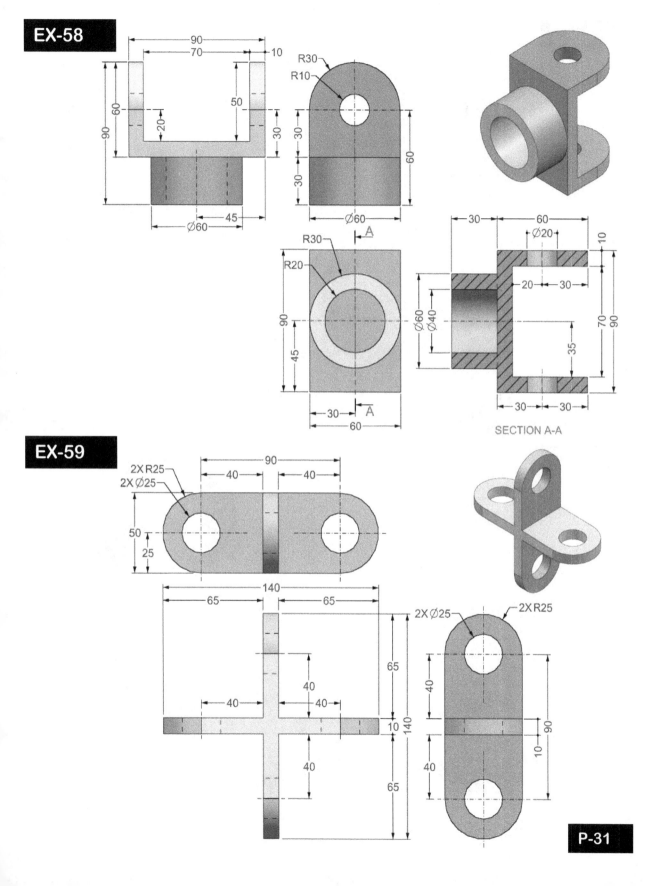

EX-58

90
70
10
90
60
50
20
30
Ø60
45

R30
R10
30
30
60
30
Ø60
A

R30
R20
90
45
30
A
60

30
60
Ø20
10
20
30
Ø60
Ø40
70
90
35
30
30

SECTION A-A

EX-59

2X R25
2X Ø25
90
40
40
50
25

140
65
65
65
40
40
140
10
40
65

2X Ø25
2X R25
40
90
40
10

P-31

EX-60

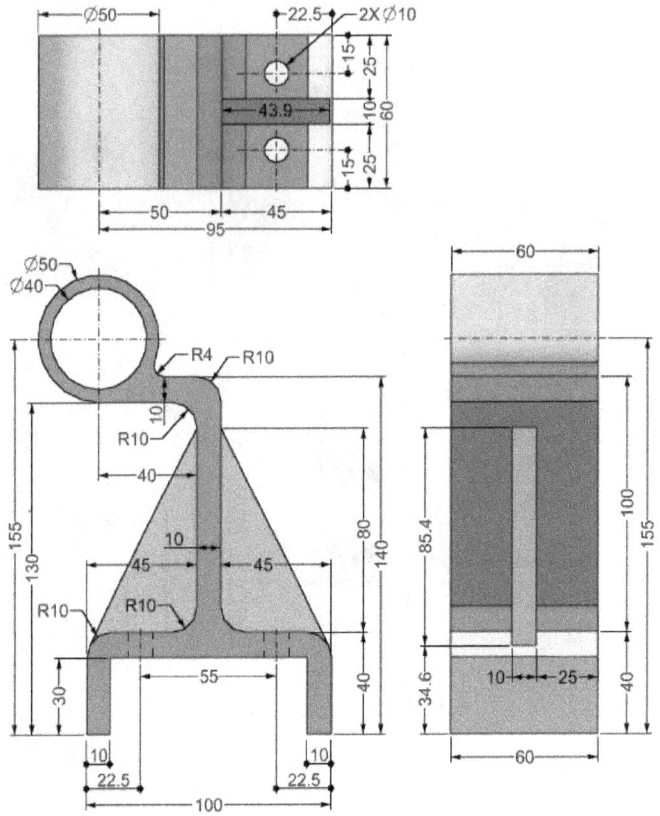

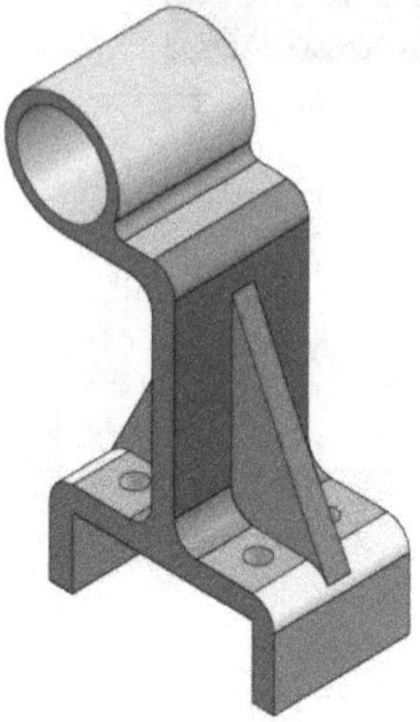

EX-61

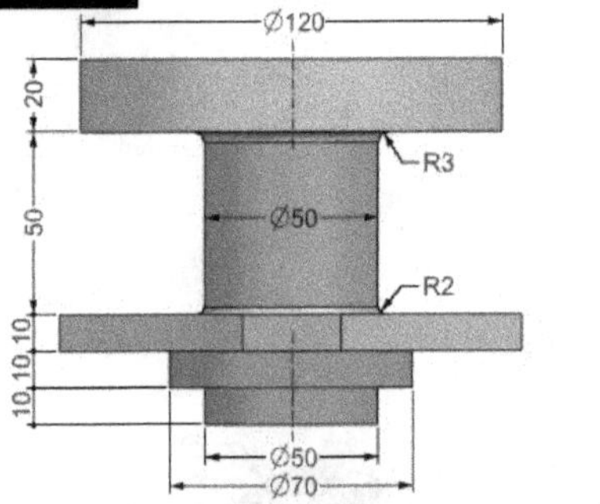

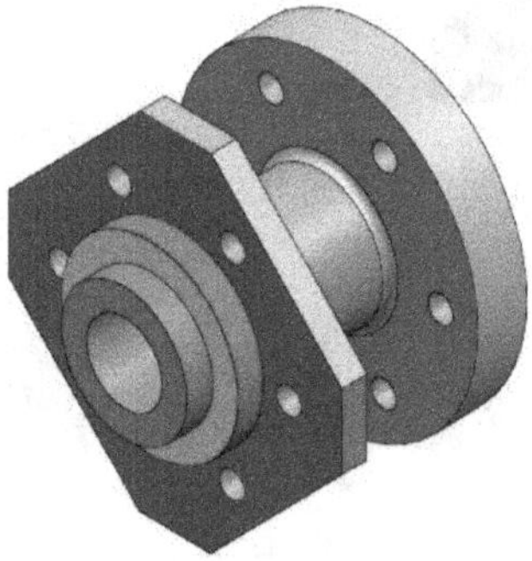

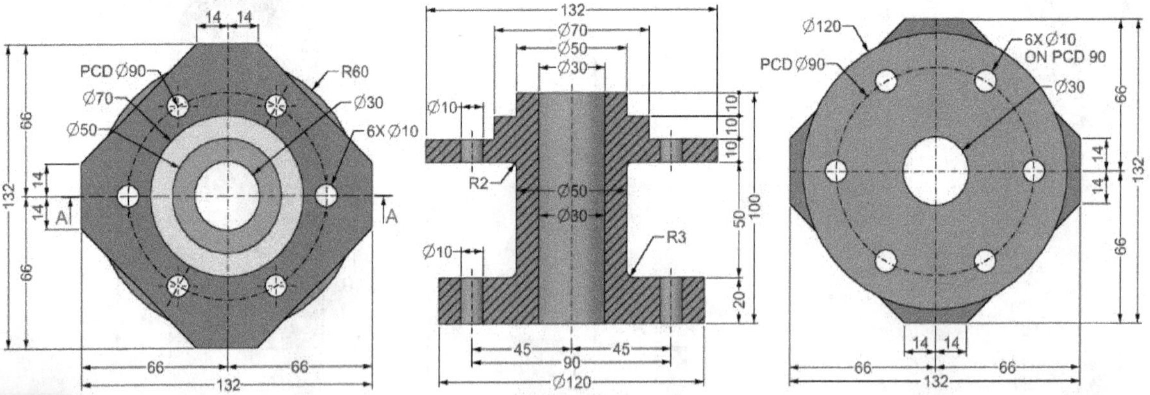

P-32

SECTION A-A

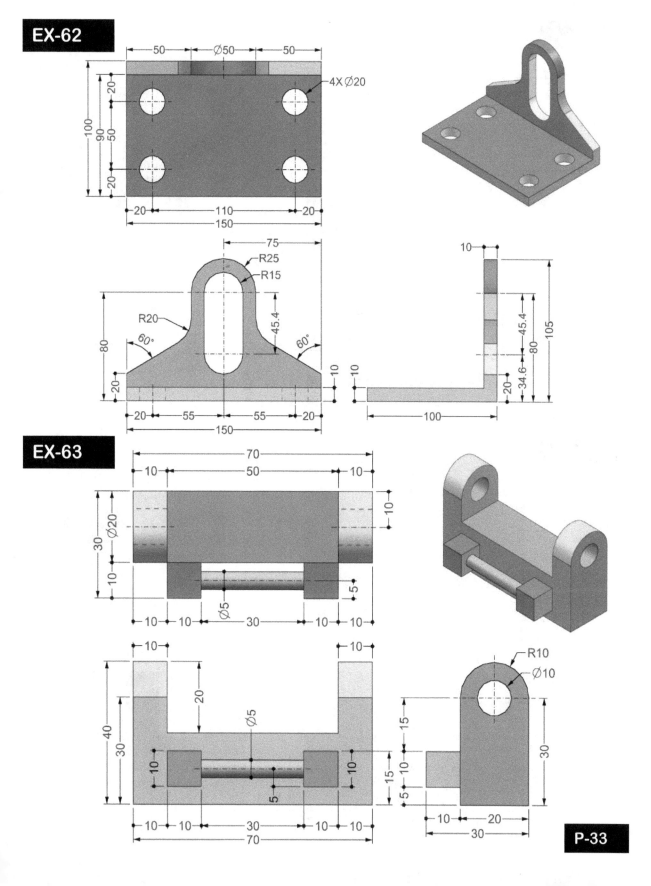

EX-62

50 Ø50 50

4X Ø20

20
100
90
50
20

20 110 20
150

75
R25
R15

R20
60° 60°

80
45.4
20
10
10

20 55 55 20
150

10
45.4
80
105
34.6
20
100

EX-63

70
10 50 10

10

30
Ø20
10

Ø5
5

10 10 30 10 10

10 10

20
Ø5

40
30

10
10

5

10 10 30 10 10
70

R10
Ø10

15
15
10
5

30

10 20
30

P-33

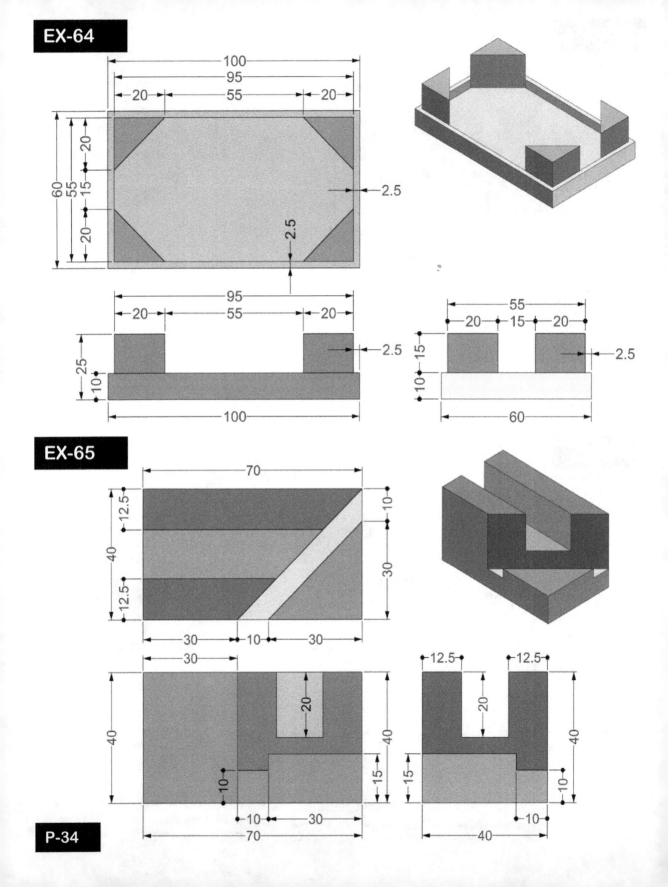

EX-64

EX-65

P-34

EX-66

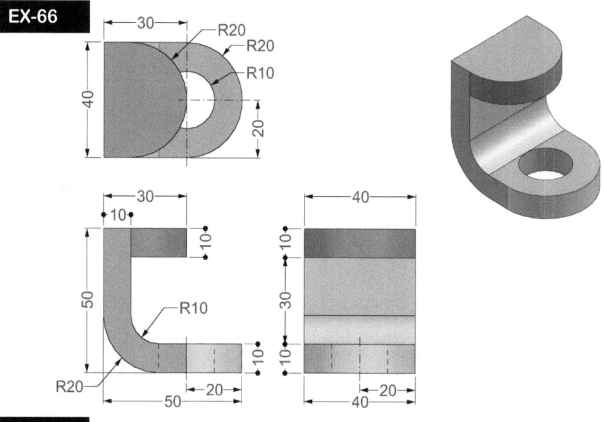

Top view dimensions: 30, R20, R20, R10, 40, 20

Front view dimensions: 30, 10, 10, 50, R10, R20, 50, 20, 10

Side view dimensions: 40, 10, 30, 10, 20, 40

EX-67

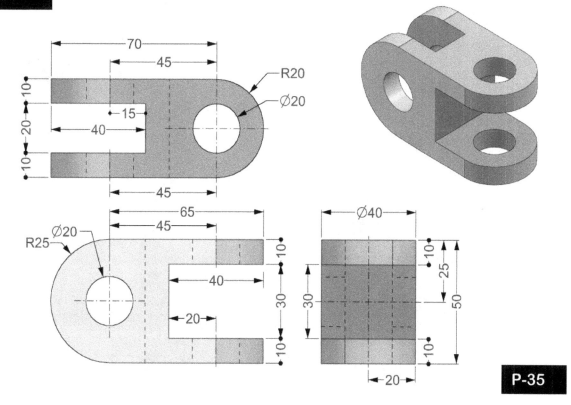

Top view dimensions: 70, 45, 10, 20, 15, 40, 10, 45, R20, Ø20

Front view dimensions: 65, 45, R25, Ø20, 40, 30, 20, 10, 10

Side view dimensions: Ø40, 30, 25, 50, 10, 10, 20

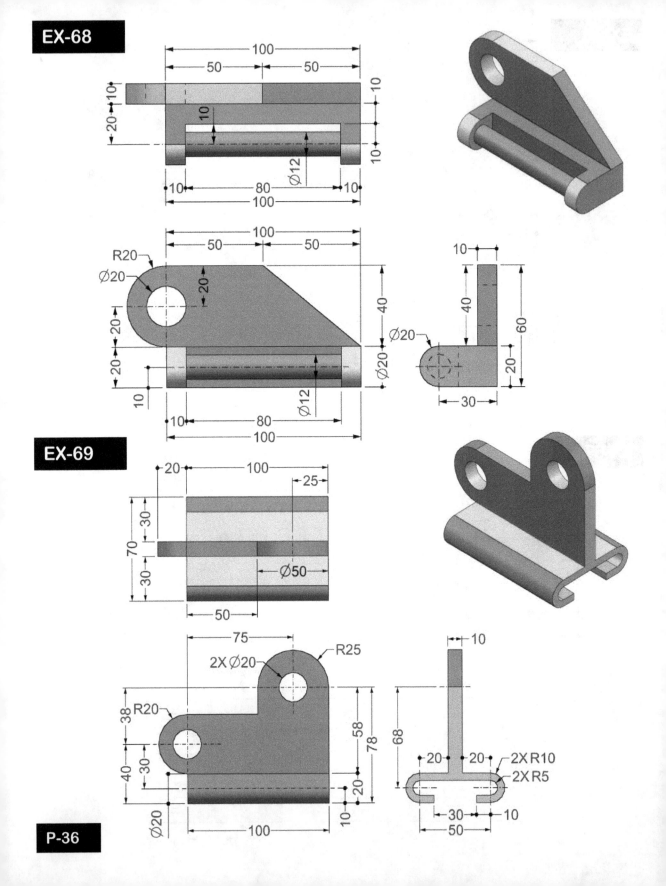

EX-68

EX-69

P-36

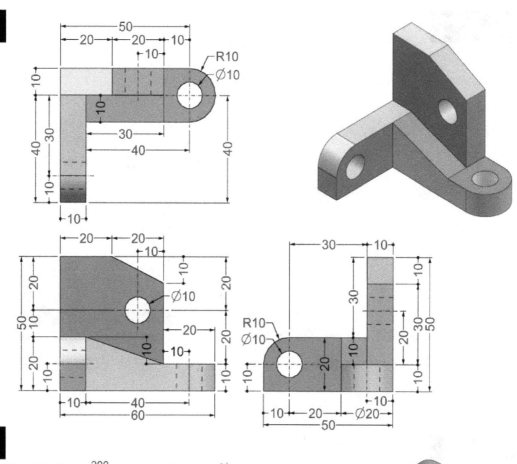

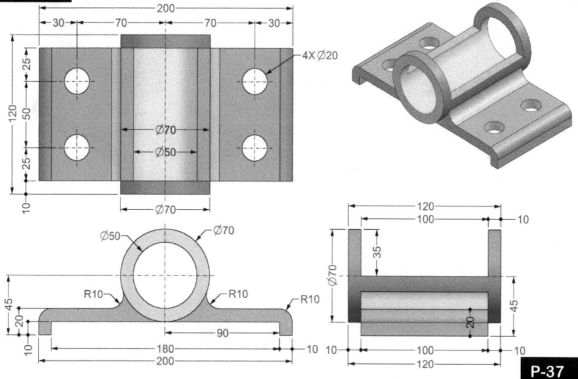

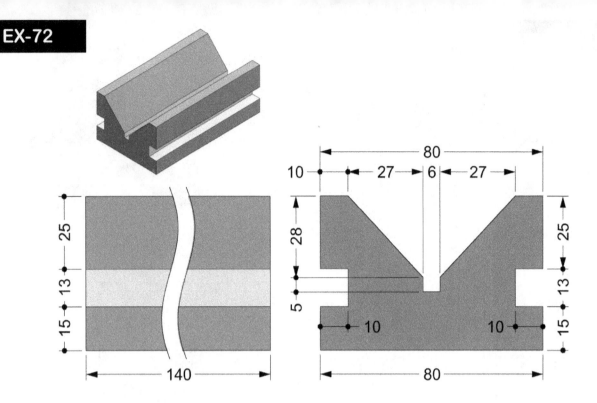

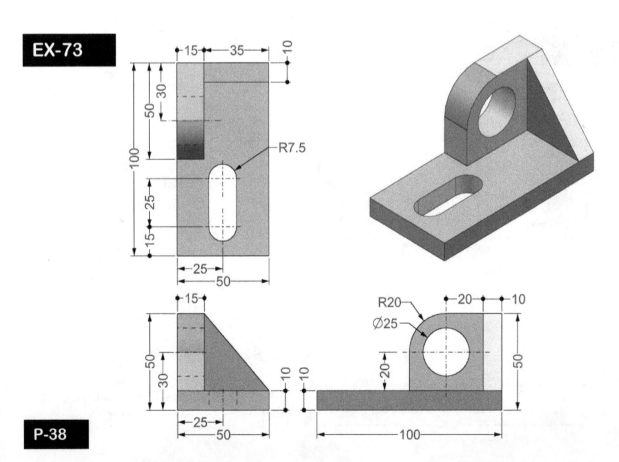

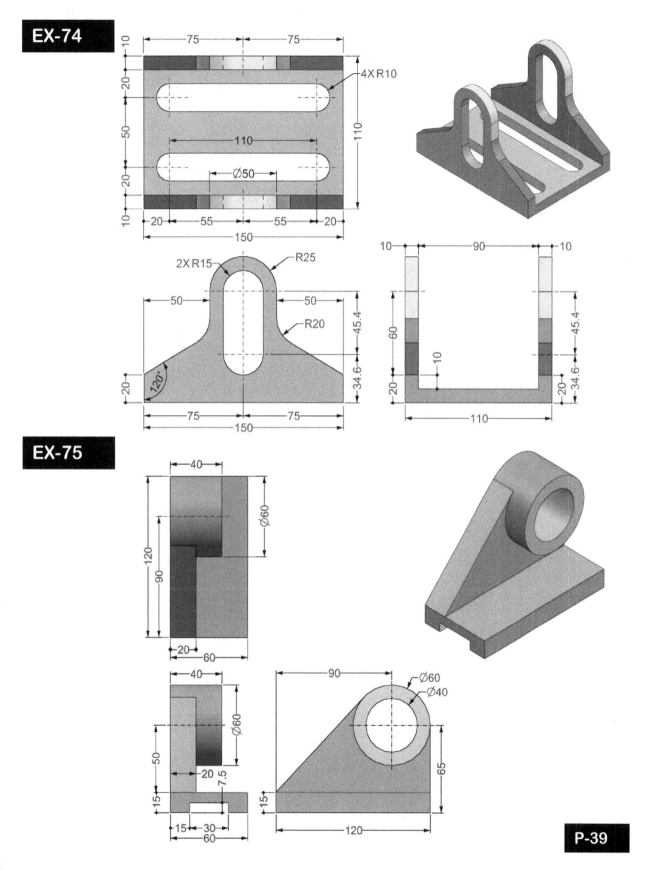

EX-74

EX-75

P-39

EX-76

120
70
R20
Ø28
40
10
20
40
10
50

70
R25
Ø30
10
15
15
10
50
70
25
20
Ø40

EX-77

R15
R25
50
R10
A
A
R5

50
Ø30
R1
30
30
20
30
30
R4
R2
Ø10
5

SECTION A-A

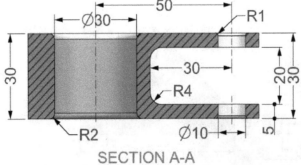

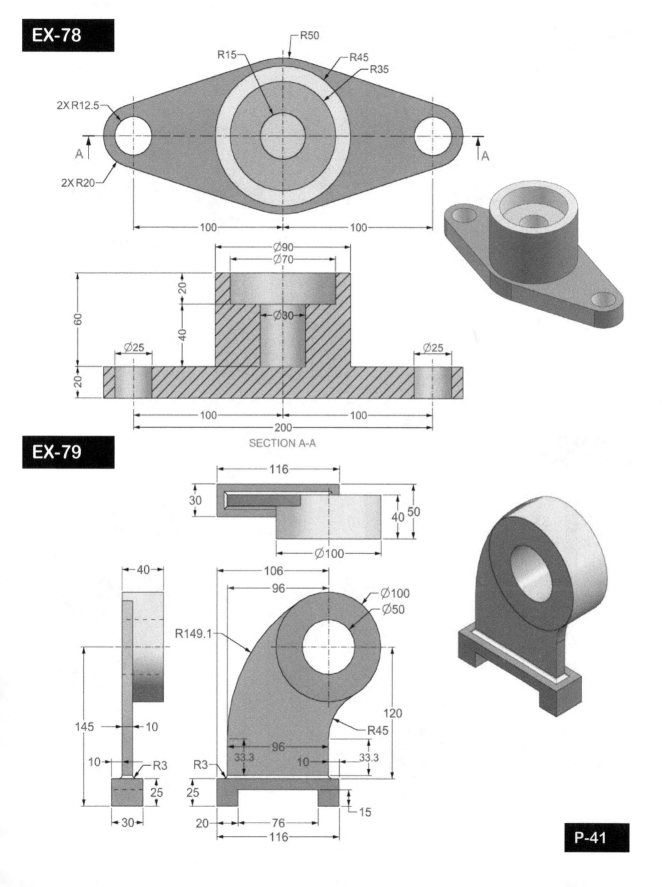

EX-78

R50

R15

R45

R35

2X R12.5

2X R20

A | A

100 | 100

Ø90
Ø70

20

60

40

Ø30

Ø25 | Ø25

20

100 | 100

200

SECTION A-A

EX-79

116

30

40 | 50

Ø100

40

106

96

Ø100
Ø50

R149.1

120

R45

145 | 10

96

33.3 | 10 | 33.3

10 | R3

R3

25

25

15

30

20 | 76

116

P-41

EX-80

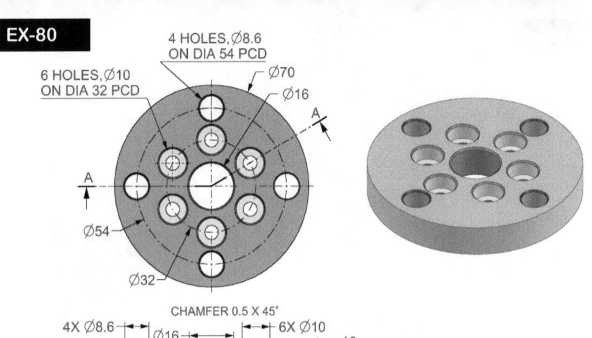

6 HOLES, Ø10 ON DIA 32 PCD

4 HOLES, Ø8.6 ON DIA 54 PCD

Ø70

Ø16

A

A

Ø54

Ø32

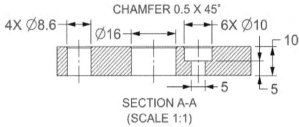

CHAMFER 0.5 X 45°

4X Ø8.6

Ø16

6X Ø10

10

5

5

SECTION A-A
(SCALE 1:1)

EX-81

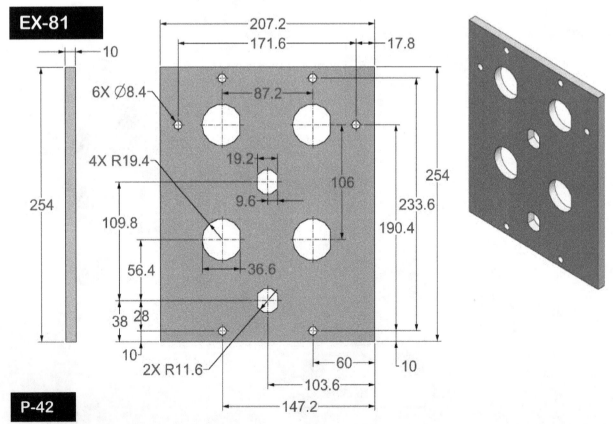

10

6X Ø8.4

207.2

171.6

17.8

87.2

4X R19.4

19.2

9.6

106

254

233.6

190.4

254

109.8

56.4

36.6

38 28

10

2X R11.6

60

10

103.6

147.2

EX-82

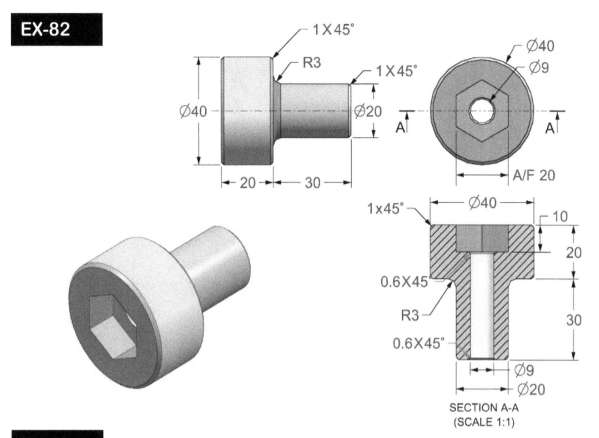

1×45°
R3
1×45°
Ø40
Ø20
20
30

Ø40
Ø9
A
A
A/F 20

1x45°
0.6X45
R3
0.6X45°
Ø40
10
20
30
Ø9
Ø20

SECTION A-A
(SCALE 1:1)

EX-83

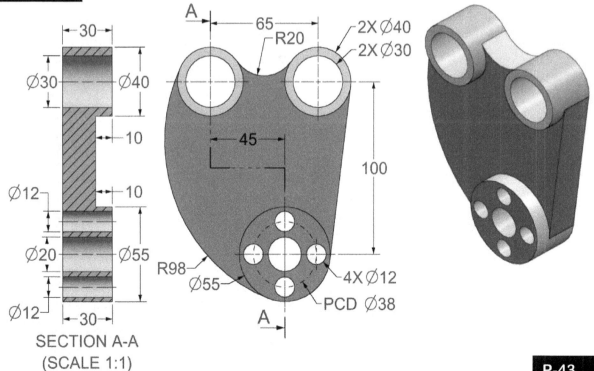

30
Ø30
Ø40
10
10
Ø12
Ø20
Ø55
Ø12
30

SECTION A-A
(SCALE 1:1)

A
65
R20
2X Ø40
2X Ø30
45
100
R98
Ø55
4X Ø12
PCD Ø38
A

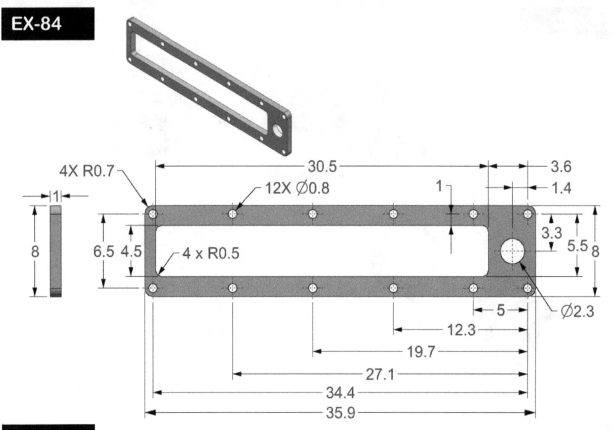

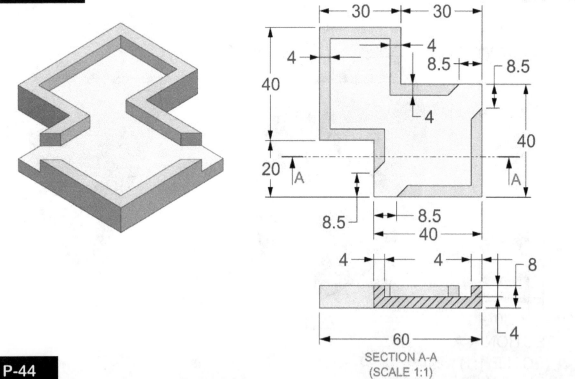

SECTION A-A
(SCALE 1:1)

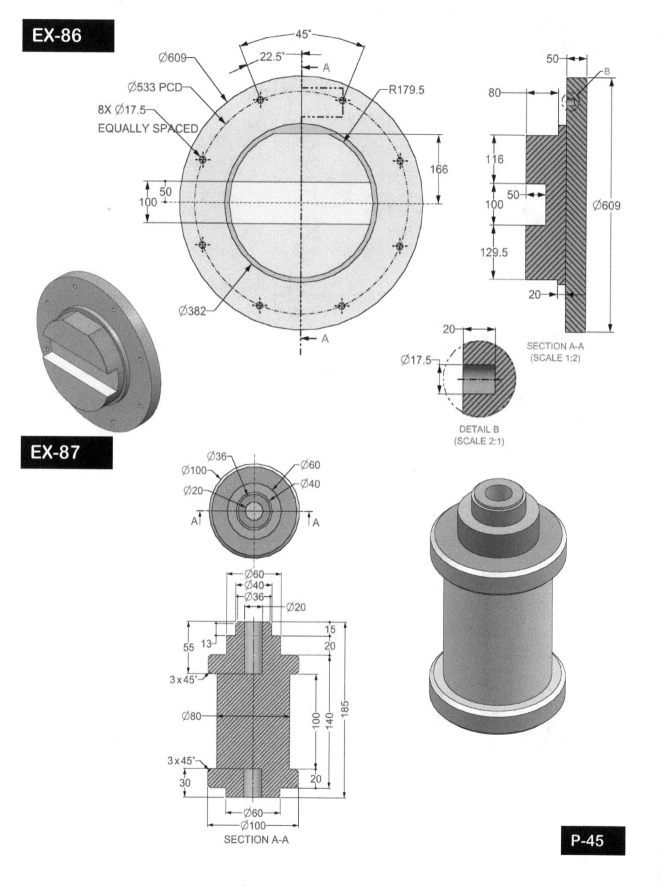

EX-86

Ø609
Ø533 PCD
8X Ø17.5
EQUALLY SPACED
45°
22.5°
A
R179.5
166
50
100
Ø382
A

50
B
80
116
50
100
129.5
20
Ø609

SECTION A-A
(SCALE 1:2)

20
Ø17.5

DETAIL B
(SCALE 2:1)

EX-87

Ø36
Ø100
Ø60
Ø20
Ø40
A
A

Ø60
Ø40
Ø36
Ø20
15
20
55
13
3 x 45°
Ø80
100
140
185
3 x 45°
30
20
Ø60
Ø100

SECTION A-A

P-45

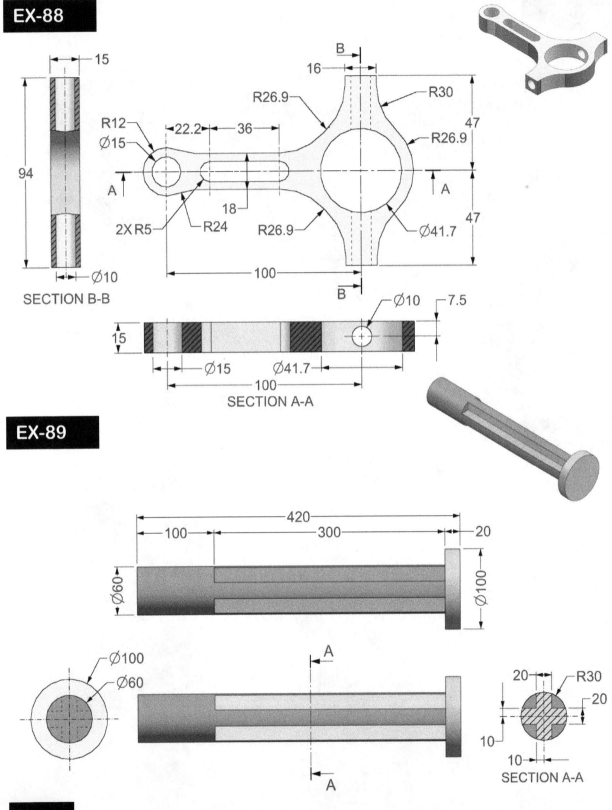

EX-88

SECTION B-B

SECTION A-A

EX-89

SECTION A-A

P-46

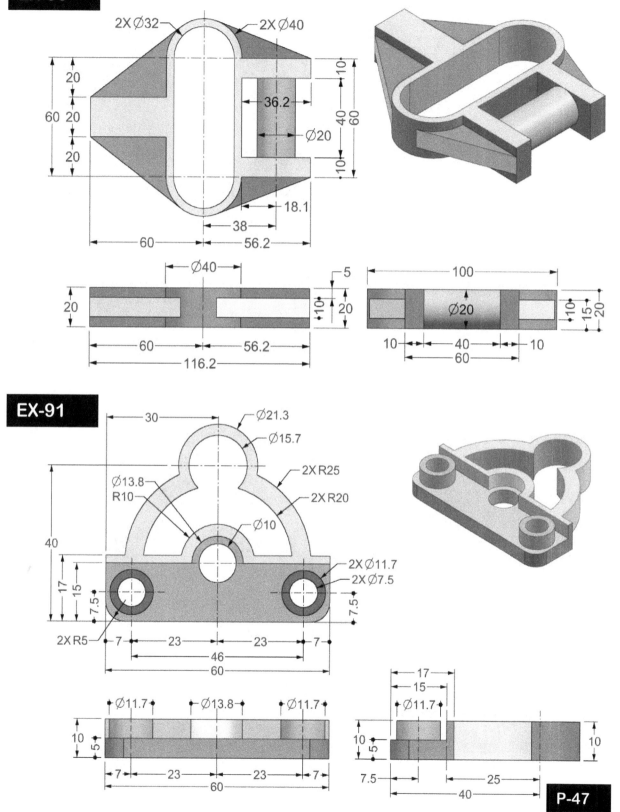

EX-90

2X Ø32   2X Ø40

20
60 20
20

10
40 60
10

36.2
Ø20

18.1
38
60   56.2

Ø40
20
60   56.2
116.2
10
20
5

100
Ø20
10 40 10
60
10
15
20

EX-91

30   Ø21.3
Ø15.7
Ø13.8
R10   2X R25
2X R20
Ø10
40
17
15
7.5   2X Ø11.7
2X Ø7.5
2X R5 7 23 23 7
46
60
7.5

Ø11.7   Ø13.8   Ø11.7
10
5
7 23 23 7
60

17
15
Ø11.7
10
5
7.5   25
40

P-47

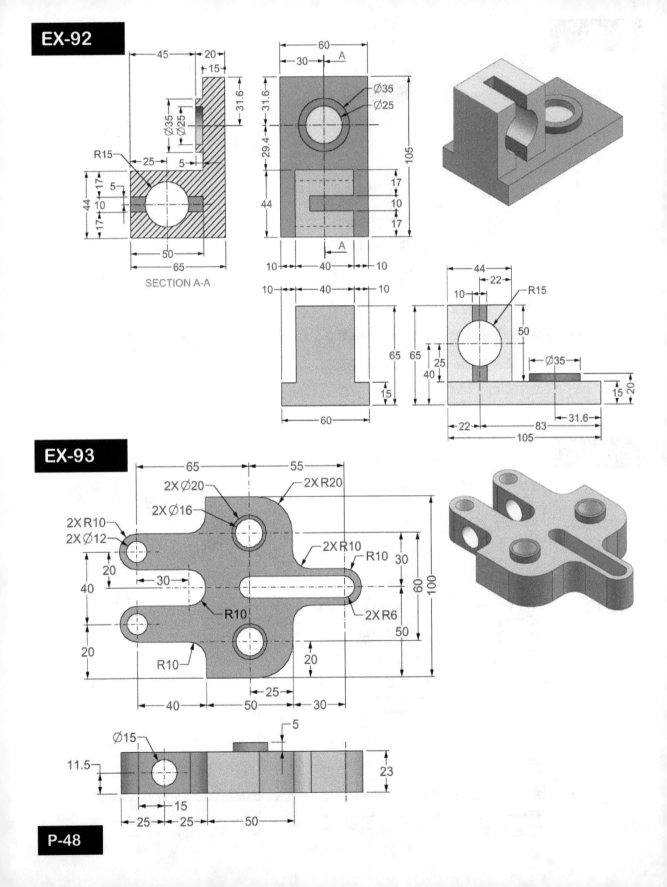

EX-92

SECTION A-A

Ø35
Ø25
R15
45 · 20 · 15
31.6
25 · 5
44 · 17 · 5 · 10 · 17
50
65

60
30 · A
Ø35
Ø25
31.6
29.4
44
17 · 10 · 17
105
10 · 40 · 10
A

10 · 40 · 10
65
15
60

44 · 22
10 · R15
50
65
25
40
Ø35
22 · 83 · 31.6
105
15 · 20

EX-93

65 · 55
2X Ø20 · 2X R20
2X Ø16
2X R10
2X Ø12
2X R10
R10 · 30
20
30 · 60 · 100
40
R10
2X R6
20
R10
25
40 · 50 · 30
20
50

Ø15
11.5
5
23
15
25 · 25 · 50

P-48

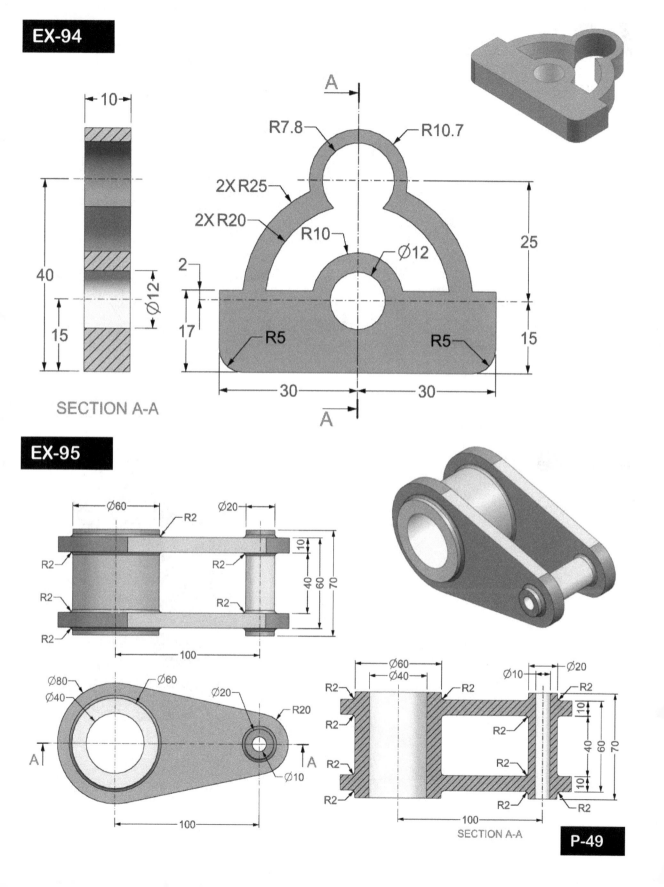

EX-94

10

40

Ø12

15

SECTION A-A

A

R7.8

R10.7

2X R25

2X R20

R10

Ø12

2

17

R5

R5

25

15

30

30

A

EX-95

Ø60

Ø20

R2

R2

R2

R2

R2

R2

10

40

60

70

100

Ø80

Ø60

Ø40

Ø20

R20

A

A

Ø10

100

Ø60

Ø40

Ø10

Ø20

R2

R2

R2

R2

R2

R2

R2

R2

10

40

60

70

10

100

SECTION A-A

P-49

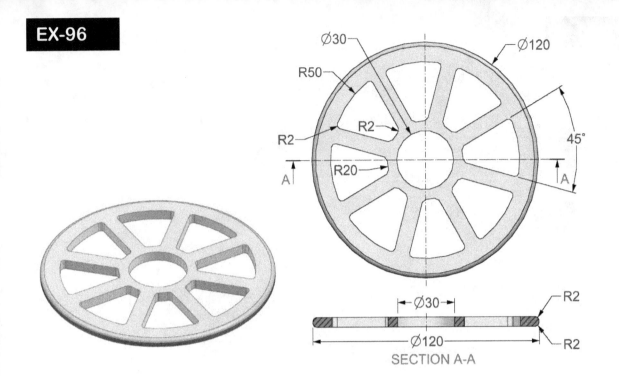

Ø30
Ø120
R50
R2
R2
R2
R20
45°
A
A

Ø30
Ø120
R2
R2
SECTION A-A

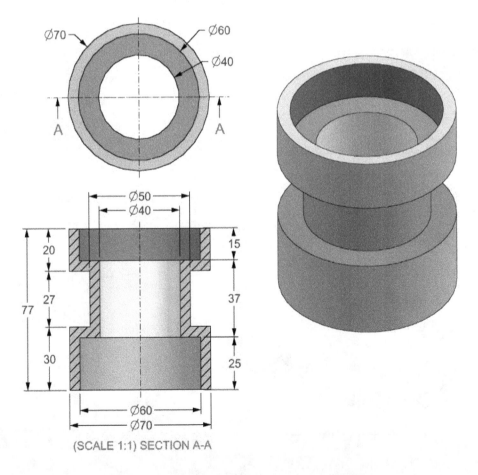

Ø70
Ø60
Ø40
A
A

Ø50
Ø40
20
15
27
37
77
30
25
Ø60
Ø70
(SCALE 1:1) SECTION A-A

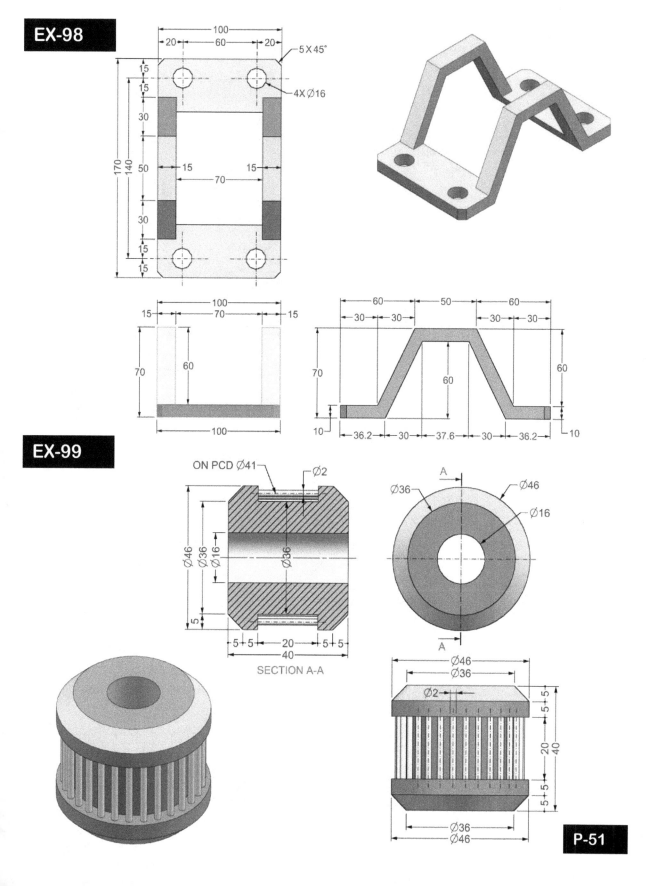

EX-98

100
20 · 60 · 20
5 X 45°
15
15
4X Ø16
30
170
140
50
15 · 15
70
30
15
15

100
15 · 70 · 15
70
60
100

60 · 50 · 60
30 · 30 · 30 · 30
70
60
60
10
36.2 · 30 · 37.6 · 30 · 36.2 · 10

EX-99

ON PCD Ø41
Ø2
A
Ø36
Ø46
Ø16
Ø46
Ø36
Ø16
Ø36
Ø36
5
5+5 · 20 · 5+5
40
SECTION A-A
A

Ø46
Ø36
Ø2
5+5
5+5
20
40
5+5
Ø36
Ø46

P-51

EX-100

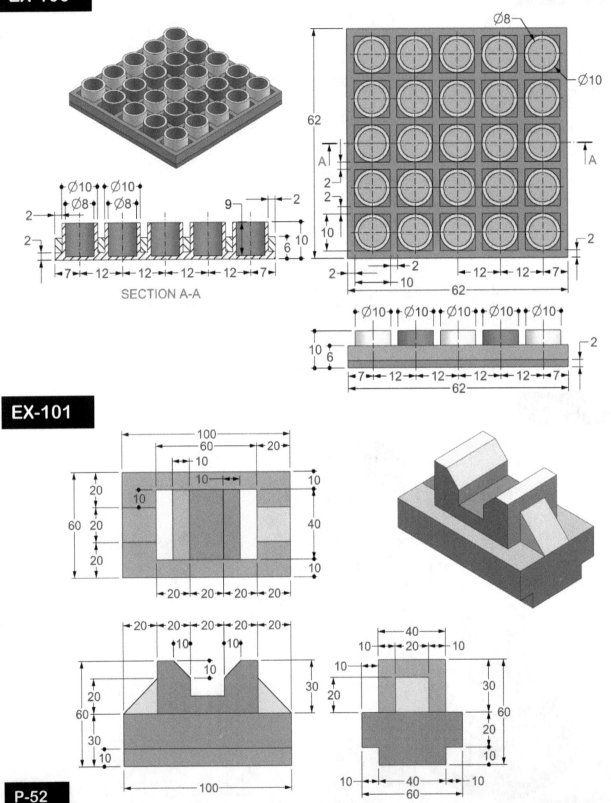

Ø8
Ø10

62

A
2
2
10

Ø10 Ø10
Ø8   Ø8
2
9
2
2

2
10
6

7 12 12 12 12 7

SECTION A-A

2
10
62

2
2 10

2 12 12 7

Ø10 Ø10 Ø10 Ø10 Ø10

10 6
2

7 12 12 12 12 7
62

EX-101

100
60   20
10
10

20
10

60 20

20

10

40

10

20 20 20 20

20 20 20 20 20
10 10
10

20
60
30
10

30

40
10 20 10
10

10

20

30
60
20
10

100

10 40 10
60

P-52

EX-102

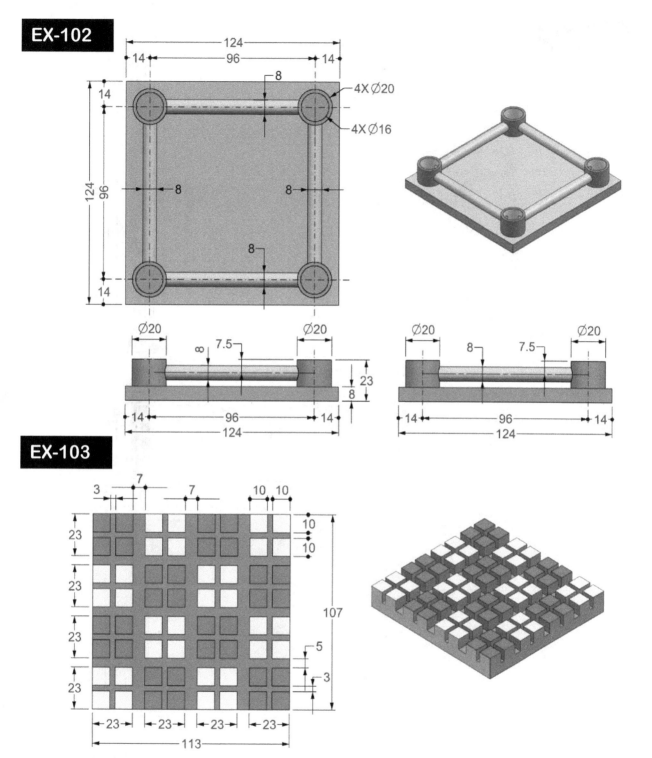

EX-103

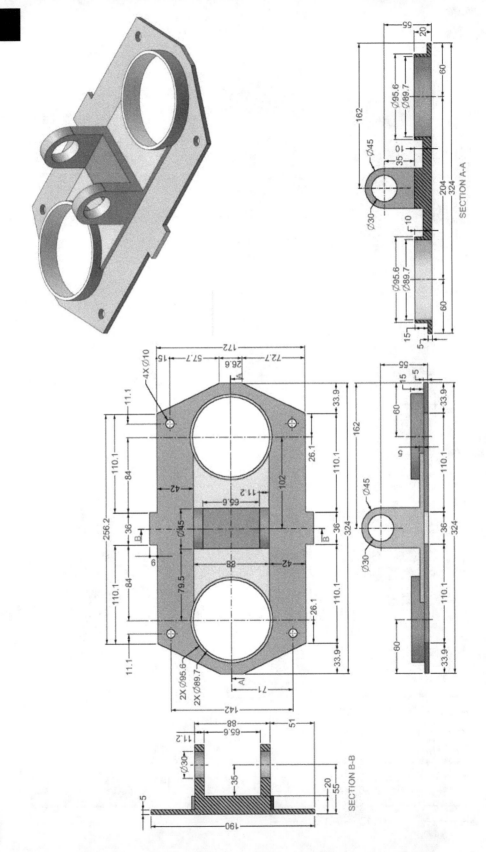

SECTION A-A

SECTION B-B

EX-105

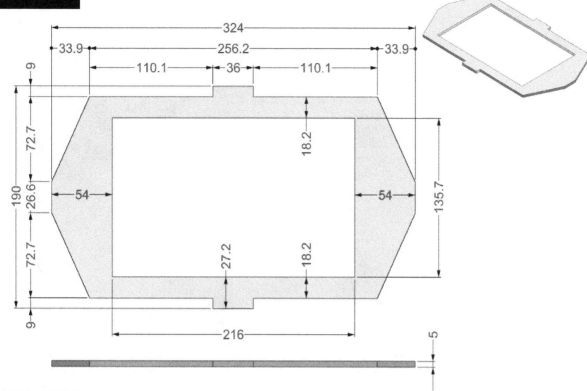

EX-106

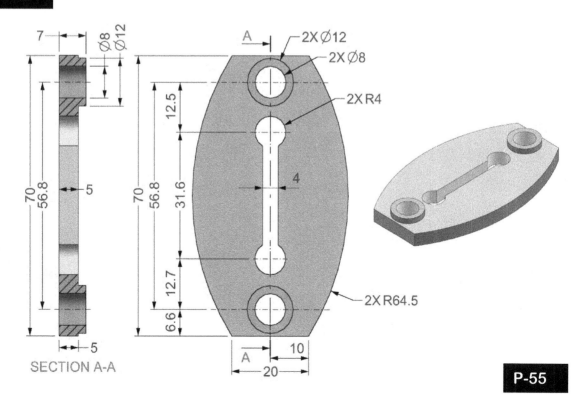

SECTION A-A

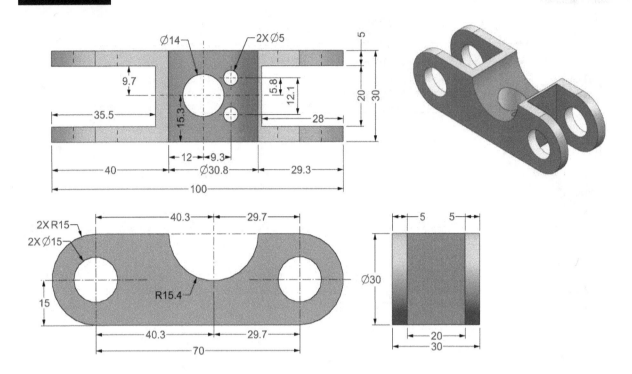

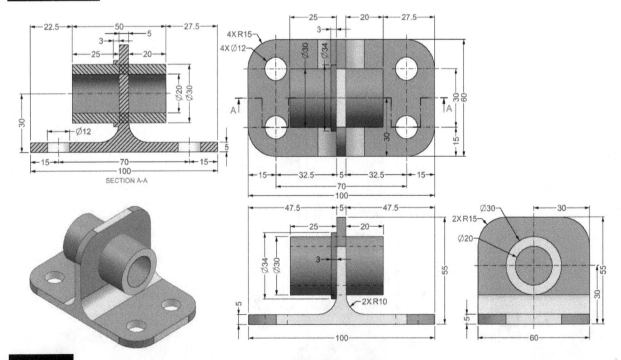

SECTION A-A

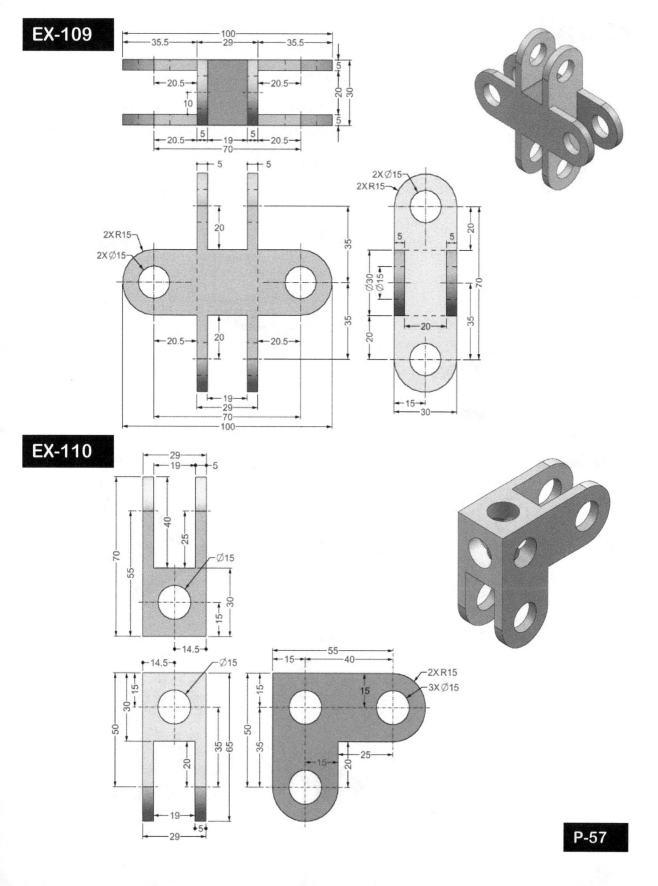

EX-109

EX-110

P-57

EX-111

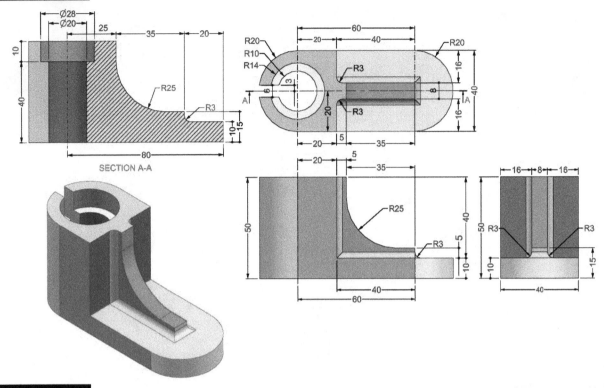

SECTION A-A

EX-112

P-58

EX-113

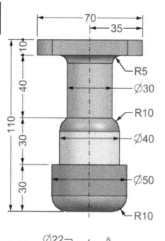

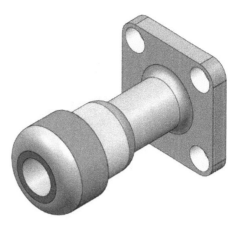

4X R10
Ø22
A
4X Ø15
Ø30
Ø50
50
70
25
10
A
25 10
50
70

70
35
10
40
110
30
30
R5
Ø30
R10
Ø40
Ø50
R10

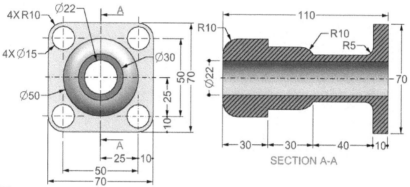

110
R10
R10
R5
Ø22
70
30 30 40 10

SECTION A-A

EX-114

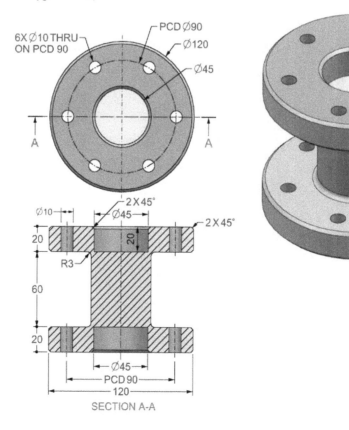

6X Ø10 THRU
ON PCD 90
PCD Ø90
Ø120
Ø45

A
A

2 X 45°
Ø45
20
2 X 45°
Ø10
20
R3
60
20
Ø45
PCD 90
120

SECTION A-A

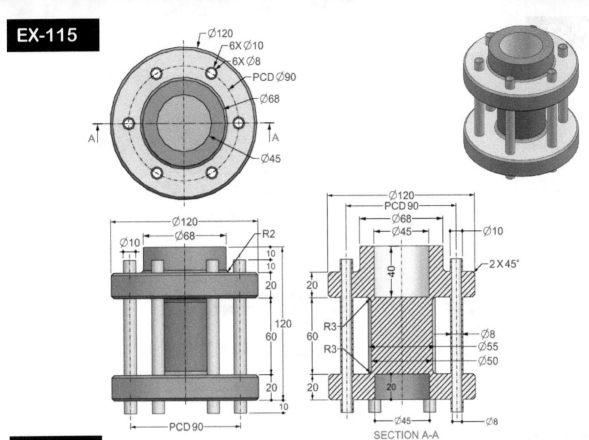

Ø120
6X Ø10
6X Ø8
PCD Ø90
Ø68
Ø45

A — A

Ø120
Ø68
R2
Ø10
10
10
20
120
60
20
10
PCD 90

Ø120
PCD 90
Ø68
Ø45
Ø10
2 X 45°
40
20
60
R3
R3
60
20
20
Ø8
Ø55
Ø50
Ø45
Ø8

SECTION A-A

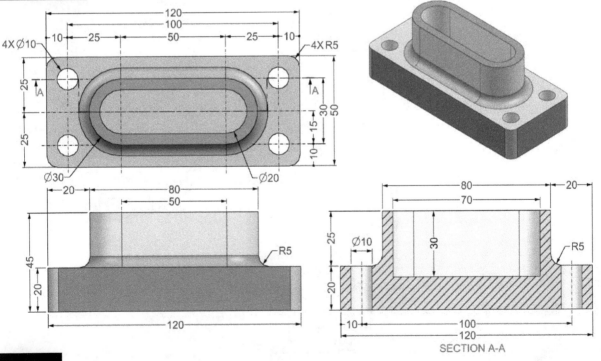

120
100
10
25
50
25
10
4X Ø10
4X R5
25
A — A
25
30
50
15
10
Ø30
Ø20

20
80
50
R5
45
20
120

80
20
70
25
Ø10
30
R5
20
10
100
120

SECTION A-A

EX-117

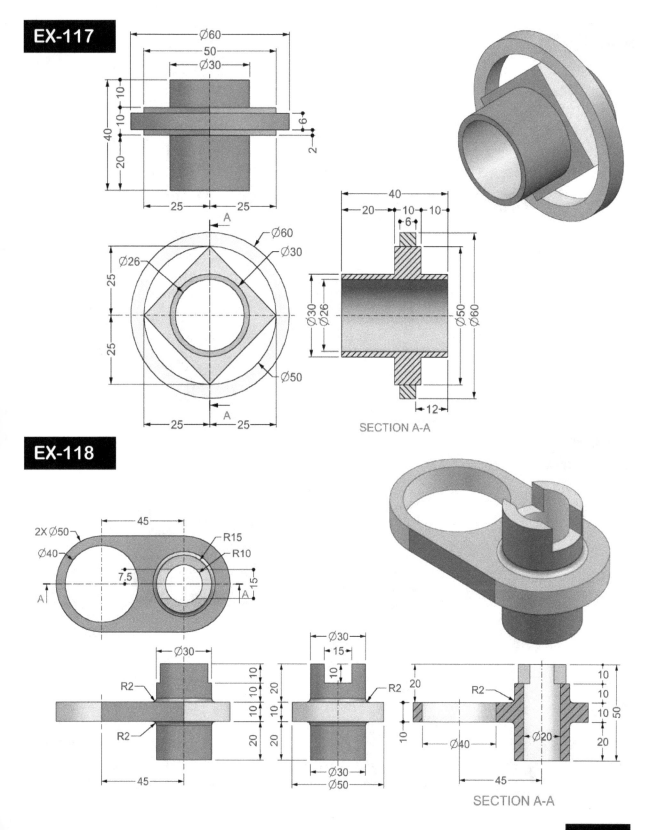

SECTION A-A

EX-118

SECTION A-A

EX-119

Ø190
Ø55

Ø140
70
2X R20
2X R25
25
50
Ø55
Ø75
Ø100
Ø180
Ø190

SECTION A-A

A
R25
25
50
Ø75
Ø190

A

Ø75
Ø190
Ø55
Ø180
Ø100

EX-120

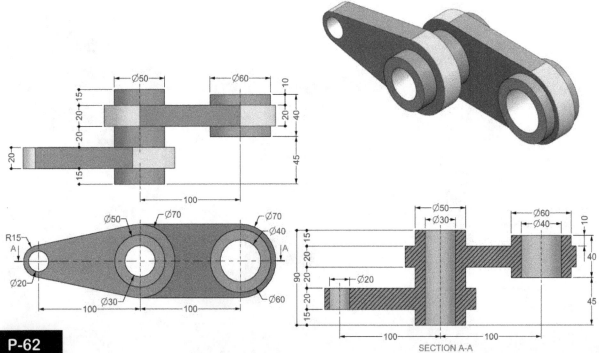

Ø50
Ø60
10
15
20
20
20
40
20
20
45
15
100

Ø50
Ø30
Ø60
Ø40
10
15
20
20
40
90
20
20
Ø20
45
15
100
100

SECTION A-A

Ø50
Ø70
Ø70
Ø40
R15
A
A
Ø20
Ø30
Ø60
100
100

P-62

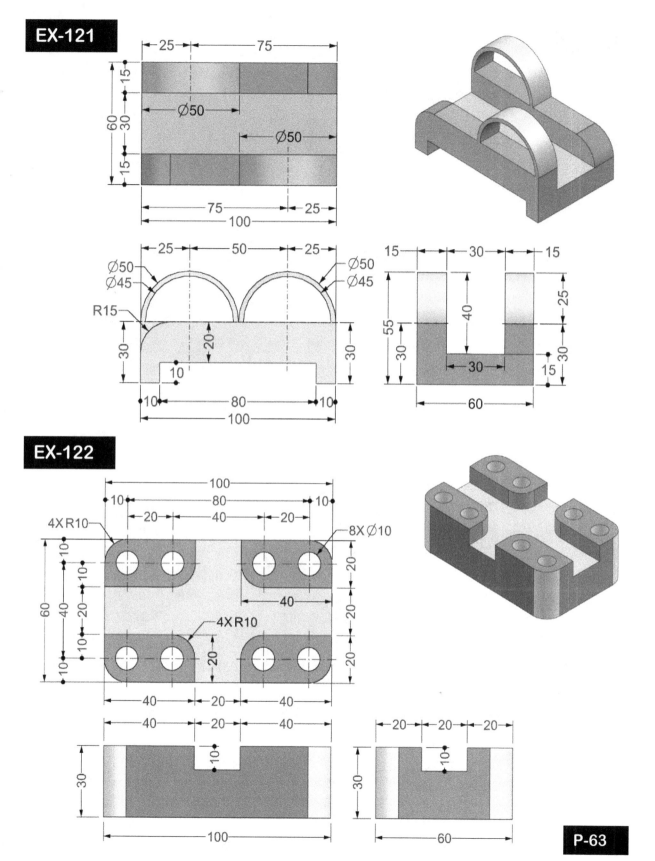

EX-121

EX-122

P-63

EX-123

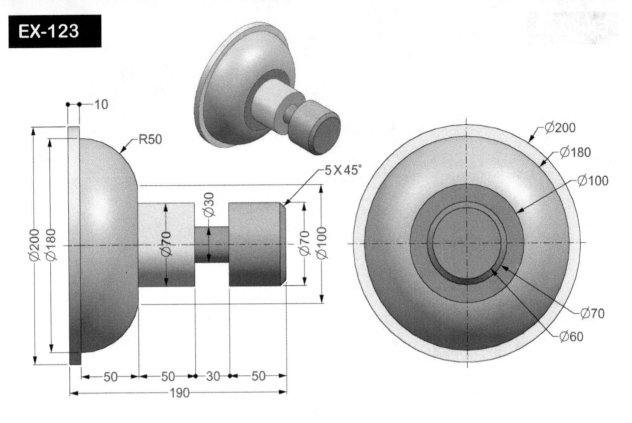

EX-124

SECTION A-A

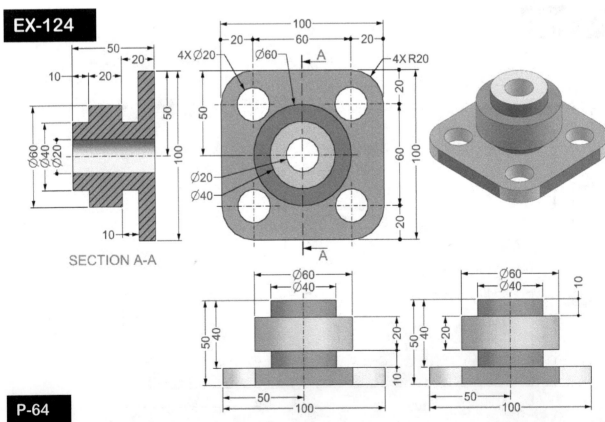

P-64

EX-125

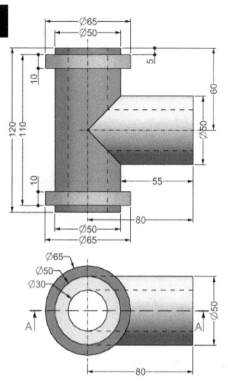

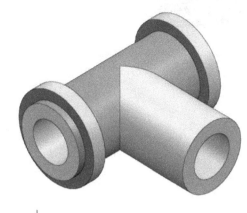

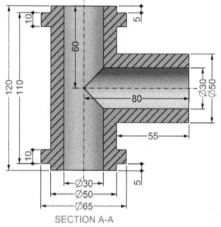

SECTION A-A

EX-126

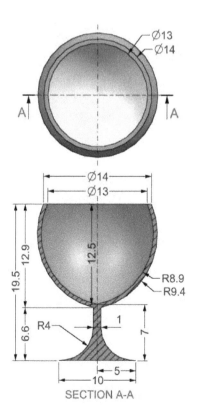

SECTION A-A

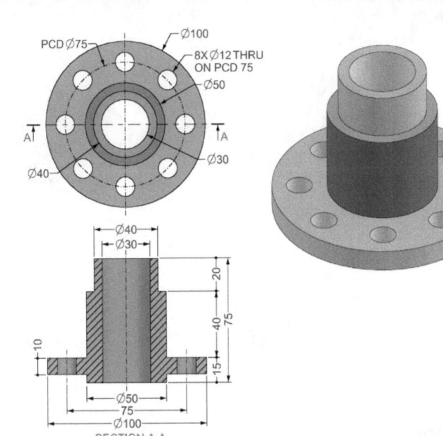

PCD Ø75
Ø100
8X Ø12 THRU
ON PCD 75
Ø50
A
A
Ø30
Ø40

Ø40
Ø30
20
40
75
10
15
Ø50
75
Ø100
SECTION A-A

EX-128

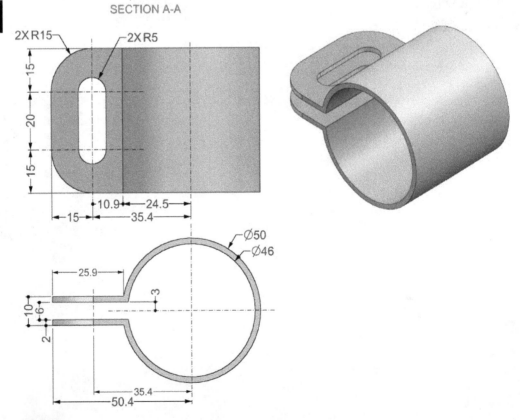

2X R15
2X R5
15
20
15
10.9
24.5
15
35.4

Ø50
Ø46
25.9
3
10
6
2
35.4
50.4

EX-129

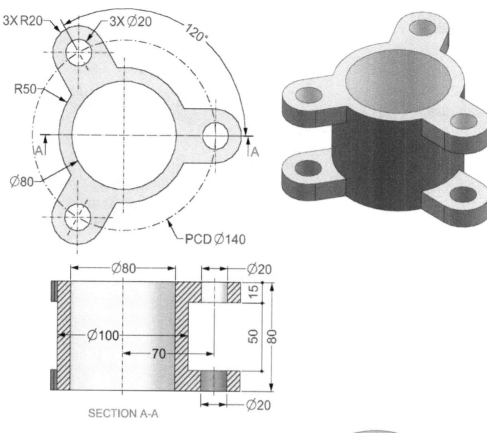

3X R20   3X Ø20   120°

R50

A   A

Ø80

PCD Ø140

Ø80   Ø20

15

Ø100

50   80

70

Ø20

SECTION A-A

EX-130

PCD Ø55   Ø70

A   A

8X Ø8
ON PCD 55
Ø30   Ø40

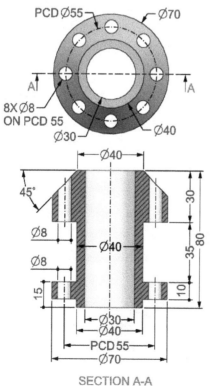

Ø40

45°

30

Ø8

Ø40   80

35

Ø8

15

10

Ø30
Ø40
PCD 55
Ø70

SECTION A-A

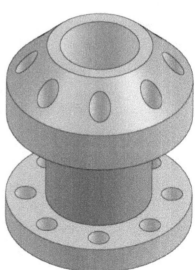

EX-131

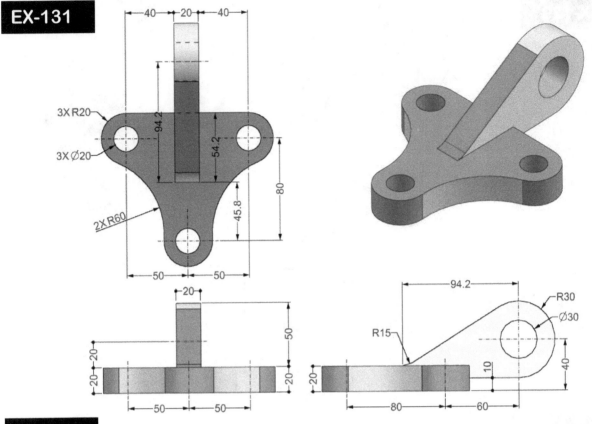

EX-132

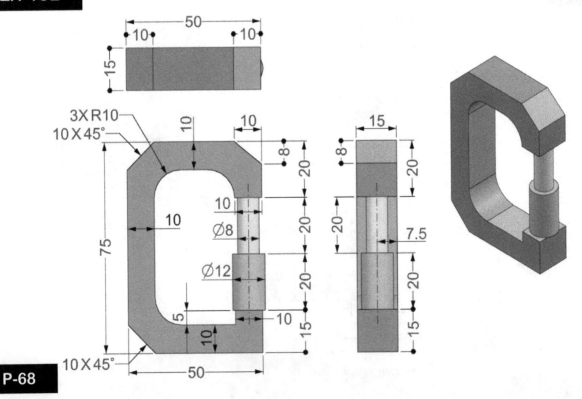

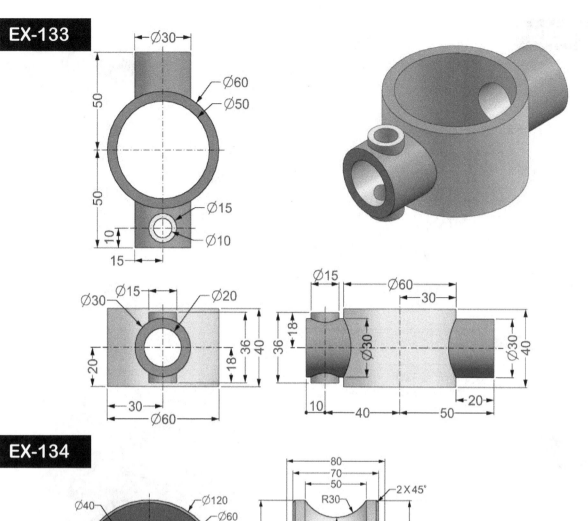

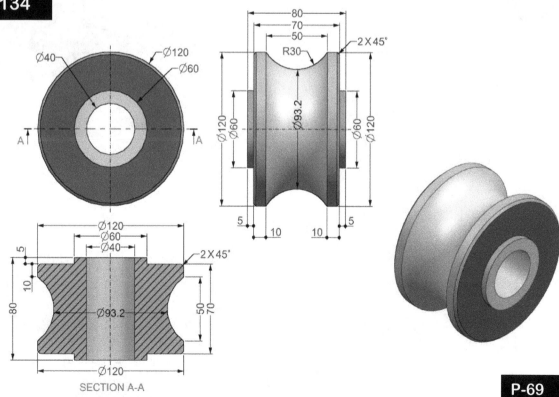

SECTION A-A

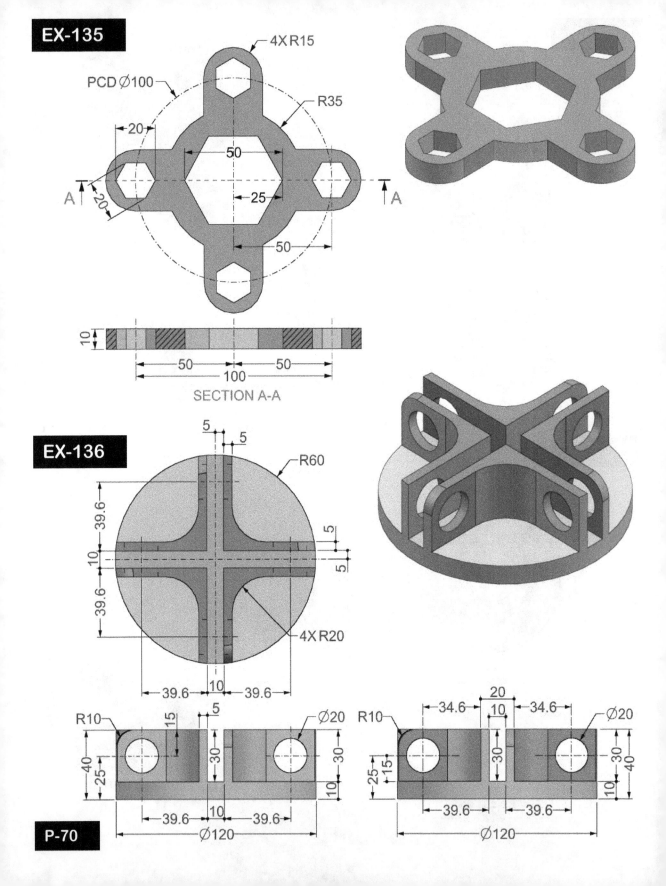

EX-135

4X R15
PCD ⌀100
R35
20
50
25
50
A
A
20

10
50
50
100

SECTION A-A

EX-136

5
5
R60
39.6
10
5
5
39.6
4X R20
39.6
10
39.6

R10
15
5
⌀20
40
25
30
30
10
39.6
10
39.6
⌀120

20
10
R10
34.6
34.6
⌀20
30
30
40
25
15
10
39.6
39.6
⌀120

P-70

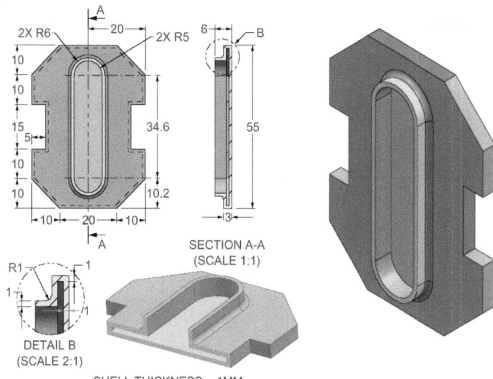

EX-137

2X R6
2X R5
20
6
B

10
10
15
5
10
10
34.6
55
10.2

10
20
10
3

A
A

SECTION A-A
(SCALE 1:1)

R1
1
1
1

DETAIL B
(SCALE 2:1)

SHELL THICKNESS = 1MM
ALL INSIDE WALL THICKNESS

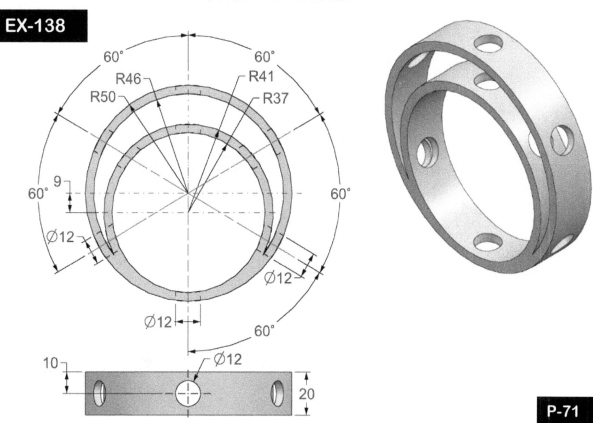

EX-138

60°
60°
R46
R41
R50
R37

60°
9
60°
Ø12
Ø12
Ø12
60°

10
Ø12
20

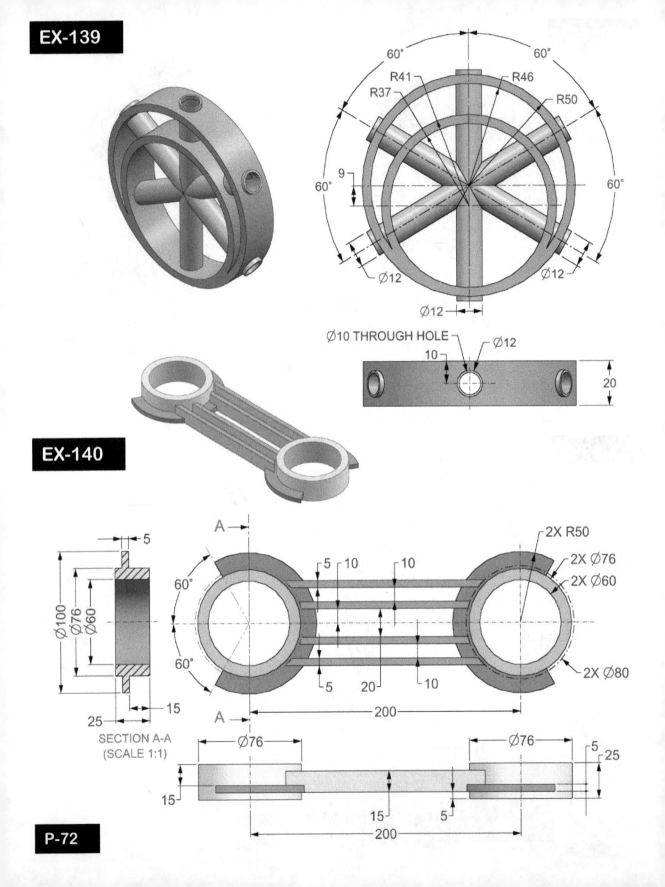

EX-139

60° 60°
R41 R46
R37 R50
60° 9 60°
Ø12 Ø12
Ø12

Ø10 THROUGH HOLE Ø12
10
20

EX-140

SECTION A-A
(SCALE 1:1)

A
2X R50
2X Ø76
5 10 10 2X Ø60
60°
Ø100 Ø76 Ø60
60°
5 20 10 2X Ø80
A
200
5
Ø76 Ø76 25
15
15 5
200

5
15
25

P-72

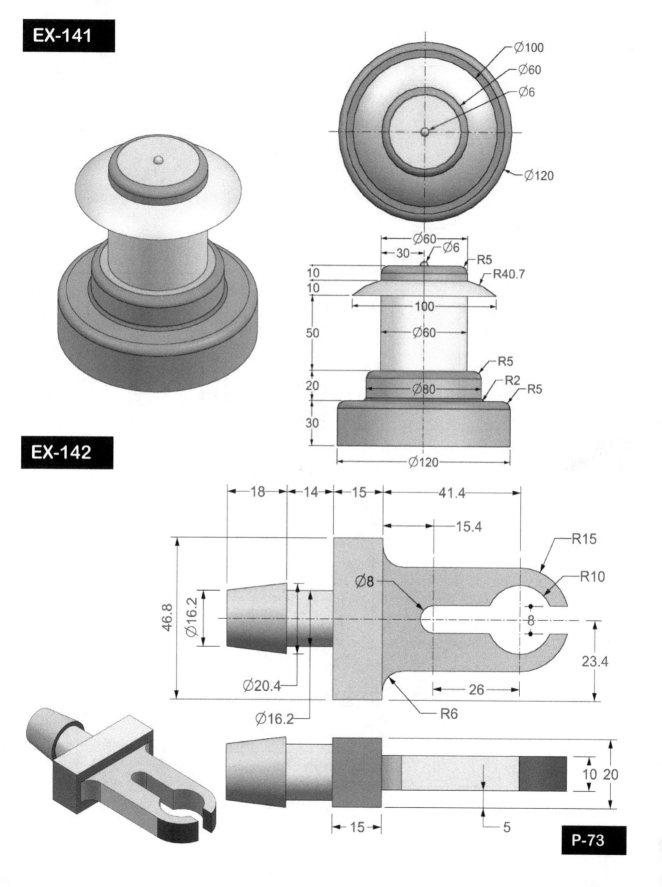

EX-141

EX-142

⌀100
⌀60
⌀6
⌀120

⌀60 ⌀6
30
R5
R40.7
10
10
100
50
⌀60
20
R5
R2 R5
⌀80
30
⌀120

18 14 15 41.4
15.4
R15
R10
46.8
⌀16.2
⌀8
8
⌀20.4
23.4
⌀16.2
26
R6

10 20
15 5

P-73

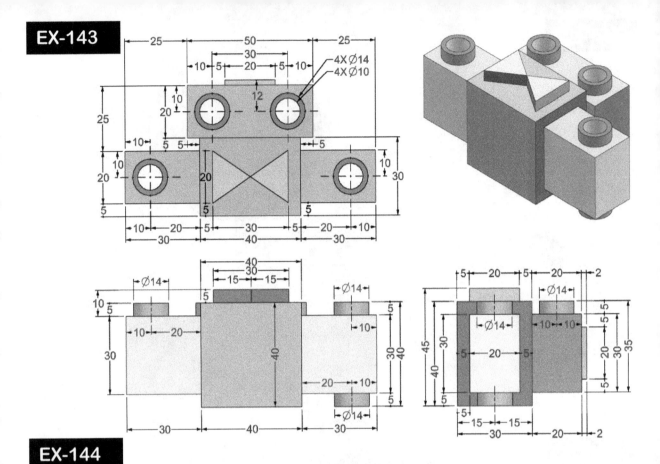

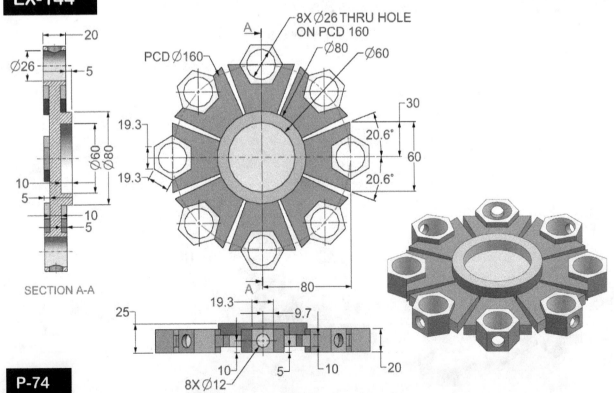

SECTION A-A

8X Ø26 THRU HOLE ON PCD 160

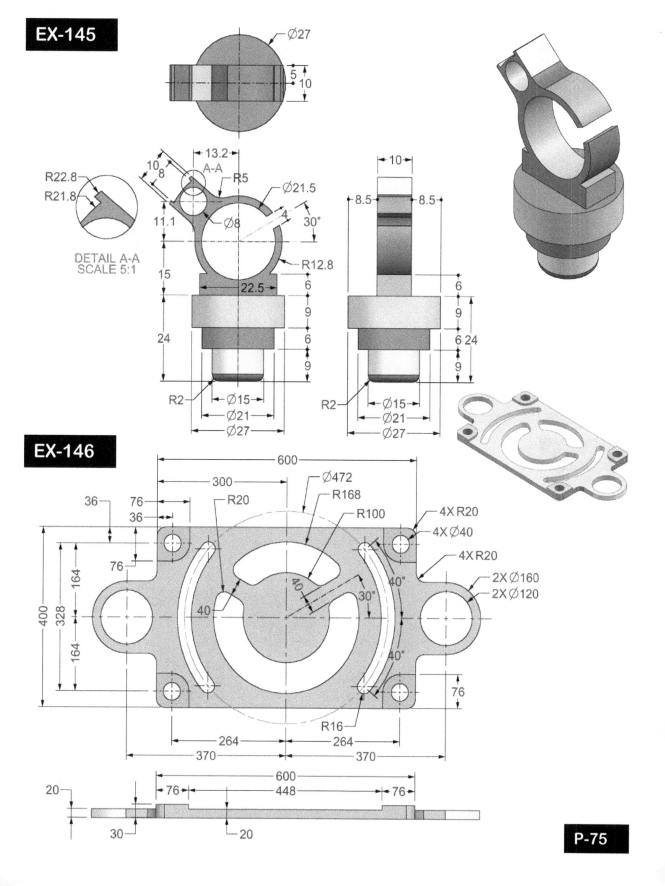

EX-145

Ø27
5
10

13.2
10
8
A-A
R5
R22.8
R21.8
Ø21.5
Ø8
4
30°
11.1
DETAIL A-A
SCALE 5:1
R12.8
15
22.5
6
9
24
6
9
R2
Ø15
Ø21
Ø27

10
8.5
8.5
6
9
6 24
9
R2
Ø15
Ø21
Ø27

EX-146

600
300
Ø472
R168
R100
4X R20
4X Ø40
36
76
36
4X R20
76
2X Ø160
2X Ø120
164
40
40°
328
40°
40
30°
400
164
40°
76
264
264
R16
370
370

600
76
448
76
20
30
20

Ø40
120°
Ø20
120°
10
60

R10
Ø40
200
79.6
Ø20
15
R15
60

2X Ø100
2X Ø80
Ø50
R45
51.6
R40
Ø30
100
100

Ø90
Ø50
10
10
40
15
100
100

Ø90
Ø80
Ø50
Ø30
Ø80
Ø80
15
10
10
40
15
100
100

SECTION A-A

A
A

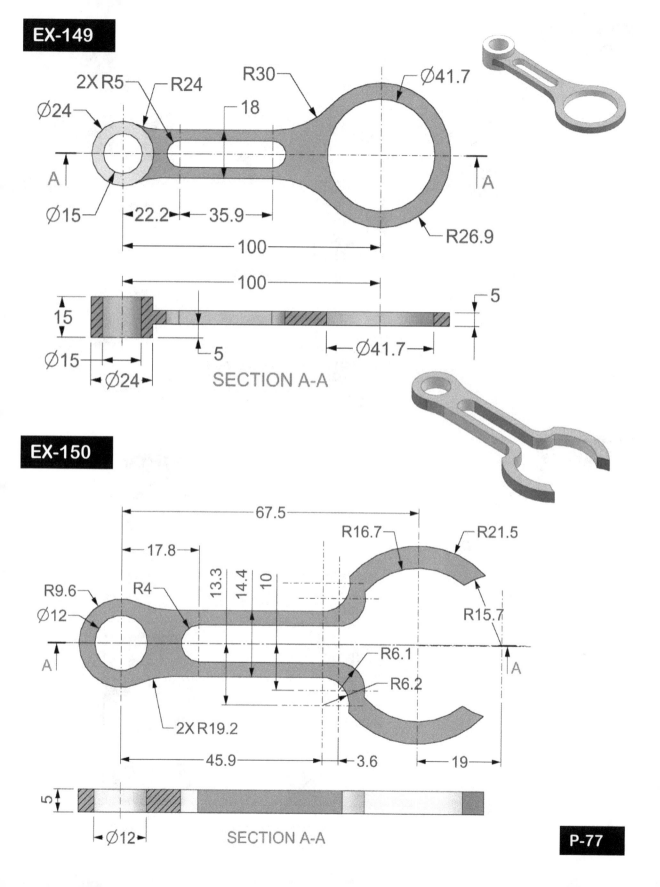

EX-149

2X R5 — R24

R30

Ø41.7

Ø24

18

2X R5

R24

Ø15

A

22.2 — 35.9

100

R26.9

100

15

5

Ø15

Ø24

5

Ø41.7

SECTION A-A

EX-150

67.5

17.8

R16.7

R21.5

R9.6

R4

13.3

14.4

10

Ø12

R15.7

A

R6.1

R6.2

2X R19.2

45.9

3.6

19

5

Ø12

SECTION A-A

P-77

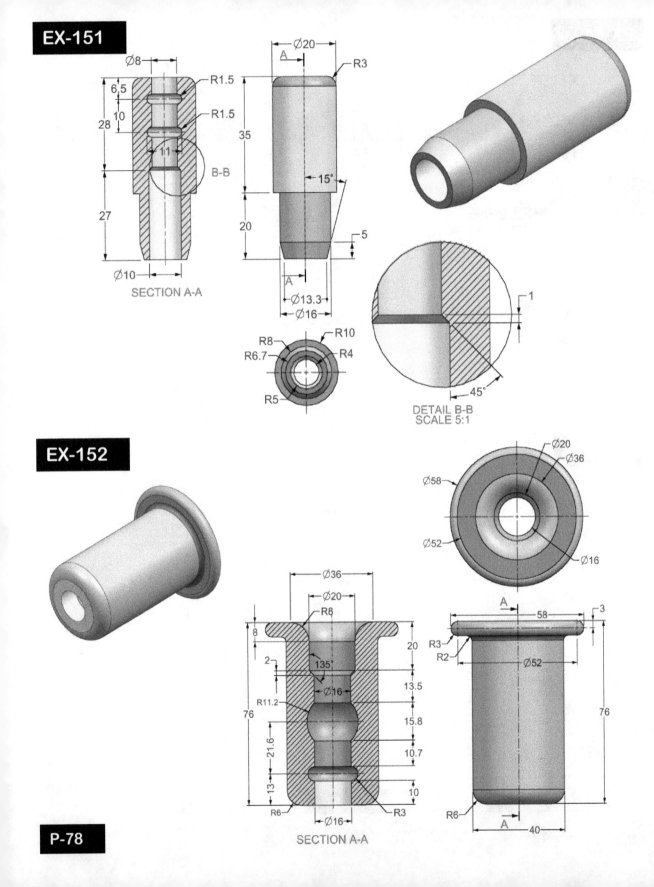

EX-151

SECTION A-A

Ø8
6.5
10
28
R1.5
R1.5
11
B-B
27
Ø10

Ø20
A
R3
35
15°
20
5
A
Ø13.3
Ø16

R8
R6.7
R10
R4
R5

1
45°

DETAIL B-B
SCALE 5:1

EX-152

Ø20
Ø36
Ø58
Ø52
Ø16

Ø36
Ø20
R8
8
2
135°
Ø16
76
R11.2
21.6
13
R6
R3
Ø16
20
13.5
15.8
10.7
10

SECTION A-A

A
58
3
R3
R2
Ø52
76
R6
A
40

EX-153

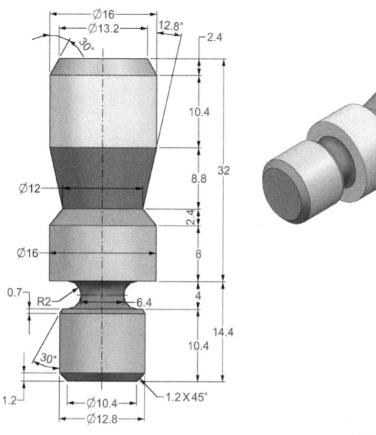

∅16
∅13.2
30°
12.8°
2.4
10.4
32
8.8
∅12
2.4
∅16
8
0.7
R2
6.4
4
30°
14.4
10.4
1.2
∅10.4
∅12.8
1.2 X 45°

EX-154

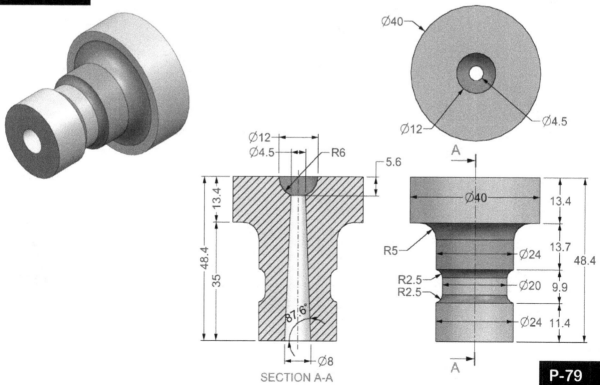

∅40
∅12
∅4.5

∅12
∅4.5
R6
5.6
13.4
A
48.4
35
87.6°
∅8
SECTION A-A

∅40
13.4
R5
13.7
∅24
R2.5
∅20
48.4
R2.5
9.9
∅24
11.4
A

P-79

EX-155

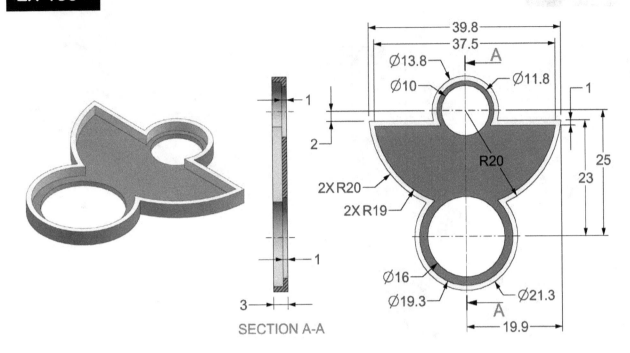

SECTION A-A

EX-156

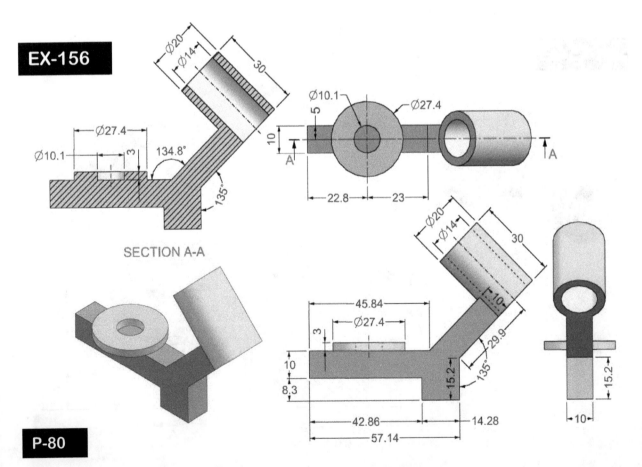

SECTION A-A

P-80

EX-157

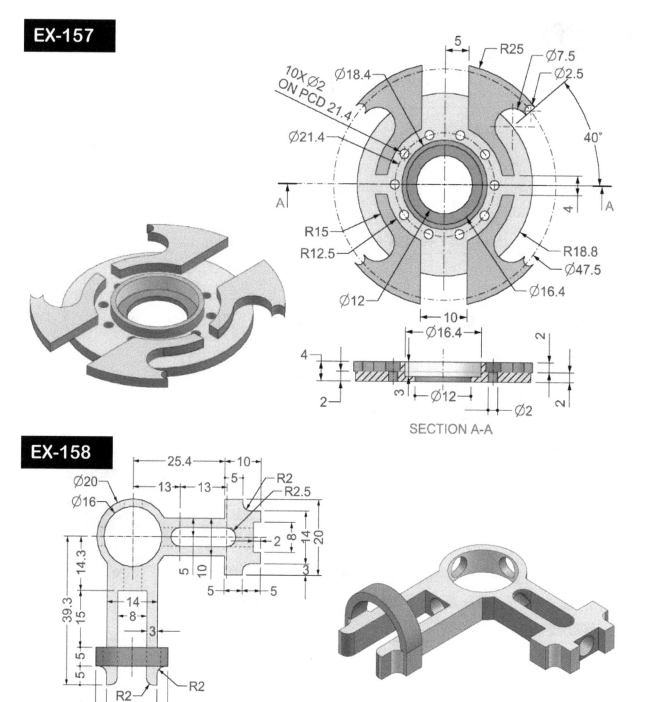

10X Ø2
ON PCD 21.4

Ø18.4
Ø21.4
R25
Ø7.5
Ø2.5
40°
R15
R12.5
Ø12
R18.8
Ø47.5
Ø16.4

SECTION A-A

Ø16.4
Ø12
Ø2

EX-158

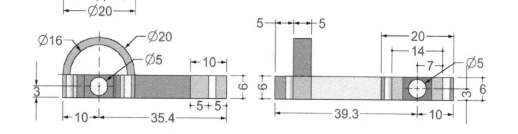

25.4
10
13
13
5
R2
R2.5
Ø20
Ø16
14.3
2
8
14
20
5
10
39.3
5
5
14
8
3
5
5
3
5
5
R2
R2
14
Ø20

Ø16
Ø20
Ø5
10
3
5+5
10
35.4

5
5
20
14
7
Ø5
6
6
3
6
39.3
10

P-81

EX-159

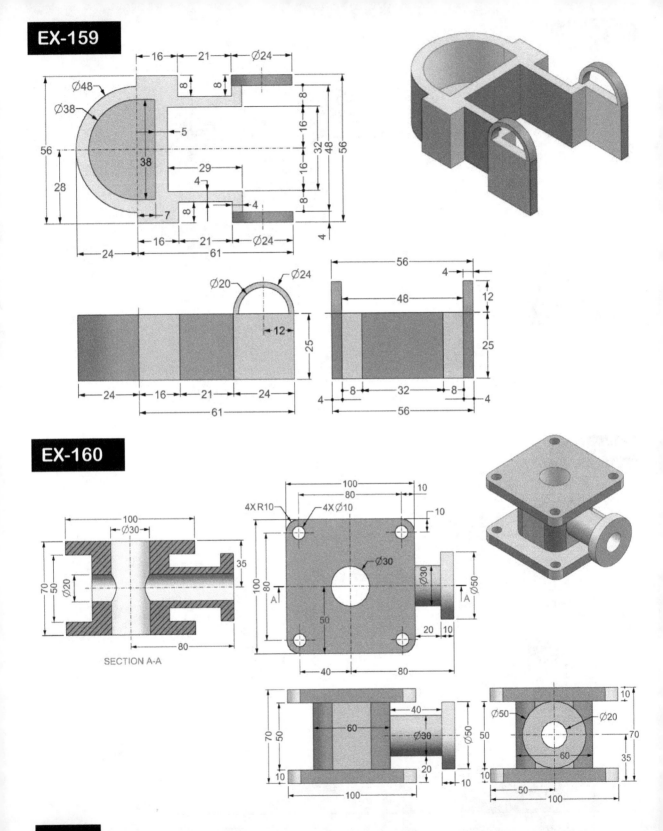

EX-160

SECTION A-A

4X R10
4X Ø10
Ø30

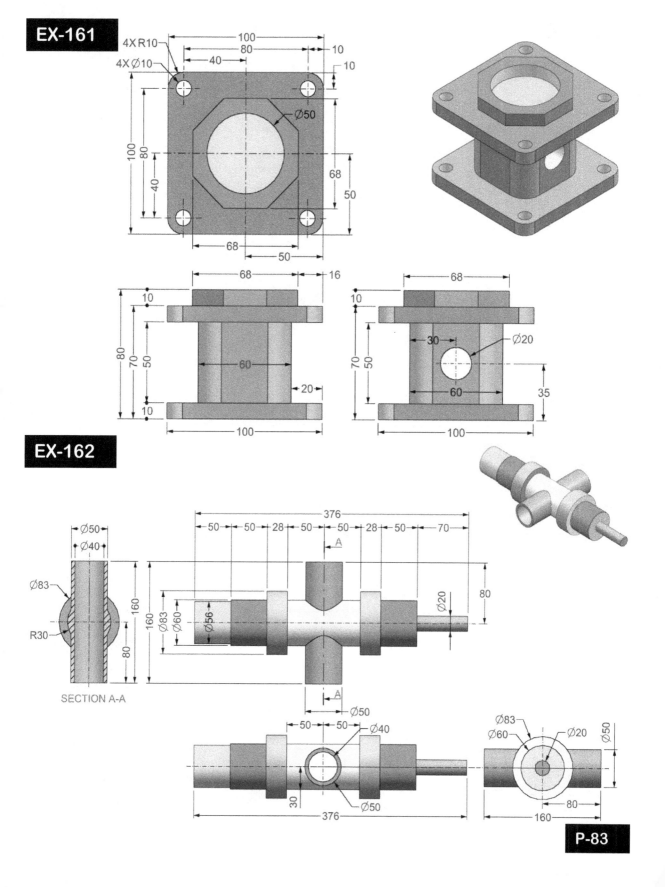

EX-161

4X R10
4X Ø10
100
80
40
10
10
Ø50
100
80
40
68
50
68
50

68
16
10
80
70
50
60
20
10
100

68
10
70
50
30
Ø20
60
35
100

EX-162

Ø50
Ø40
Ø83
R30
160
80
SECTION A-A

376
50 50 28 50 50 28 50 70
A
Ø83
Ø60
Ø56
160
Ø20
80
A

Ø50
50 50 Ø40
30
Ø50
376

Ø83
Ø60
Ø20
Ø50
80
160

P-83

EX-163

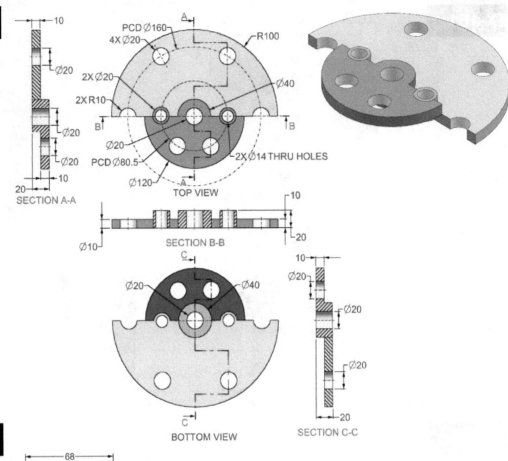

SECTION A-A

PCD Ø160
4X Ø20
R100
2X Ø20
2X R10
Ø40
Ø20
PCD Ø80.5
2X Ø14 THRU HOLES
Ø120
TOP VIEW

Ø10
SECTION B-B

Ø20
Ø40
Ø20
BOTTOM VIEW

Ø20
Ø20
Ø20
SECTION C-C

EX-164

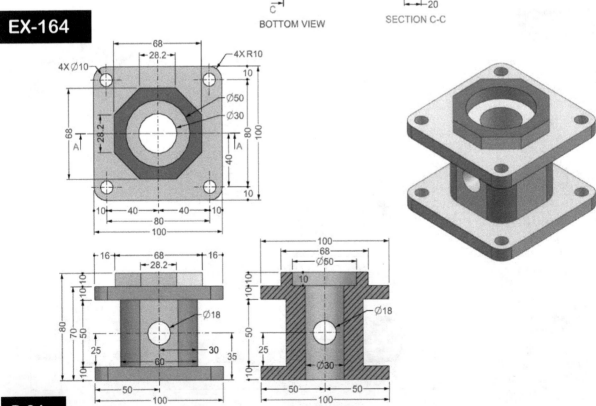

68
28.2
4X R10
4X Ø10
10
Ø50
Ø30
68
28.2
80
100
40
A
10
10
40
40
10
80
100

16
68
16
28.2
10 10
Ø18
80
70
50
25
30
60
10
50
100
35

100
68
Ø50
10 10
10
Ø18
50
25
Ø30
50
50
100
SECTION A-A

P-84

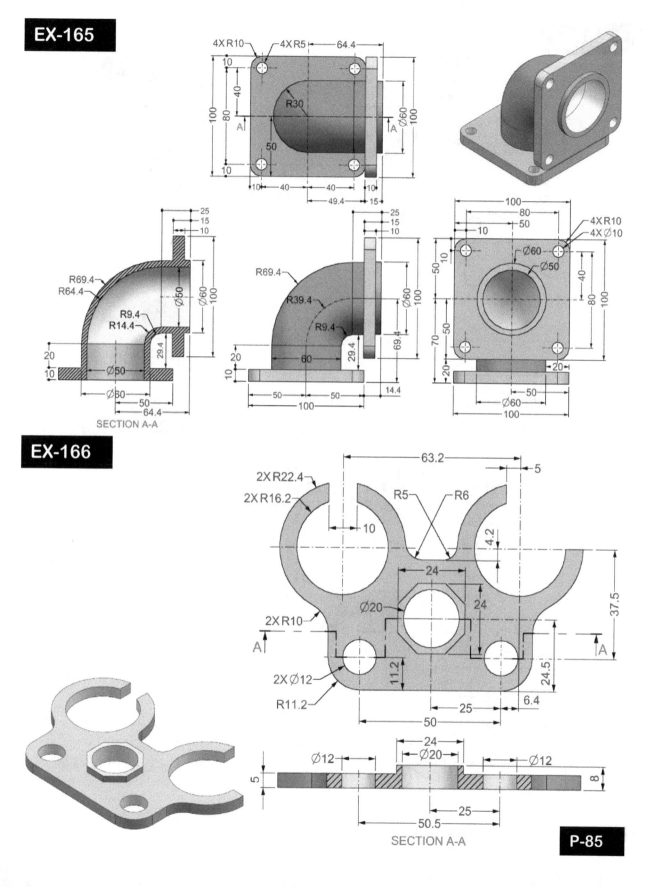

EX-165

4X R10 4X R5 64.4
10
40
80
100
R30
Ø60
100
Al
A
50
10
10 40 40 10
49.4 15

25
15
10
R69.4
R64.4
R9.4
R14.4
Ø50
Ø60
100
20
10
29.4
Ø50
Ø60
50
64.4
SECTION A-A

25
15
10
R69.4
R39.4
R9.4
Ø60
100
69.4
20
10
29.4
60
50 50
100
14.4

100
80
50
10
Ø60
Ø50
4X R10
4X Ø10
50
10
40
80
100
70
50
20
20
50
Ø60
100

EX-166

63.2
5
2X R22.4
2X R16.2
R5 R6
10
4.2
24
Ø20
24
37.5
2X R10
A
24.5
2X Ø12
11.2
6.4
R11.2
25
50

24
Ø12 Ø20 Ø12
5
8
25
50.5
SECTION A-A

P-85

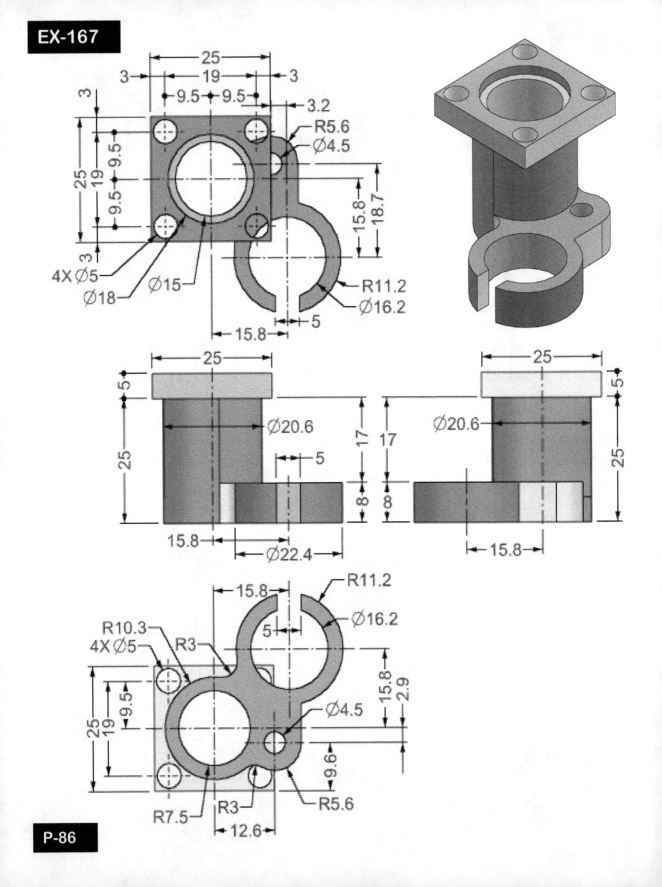

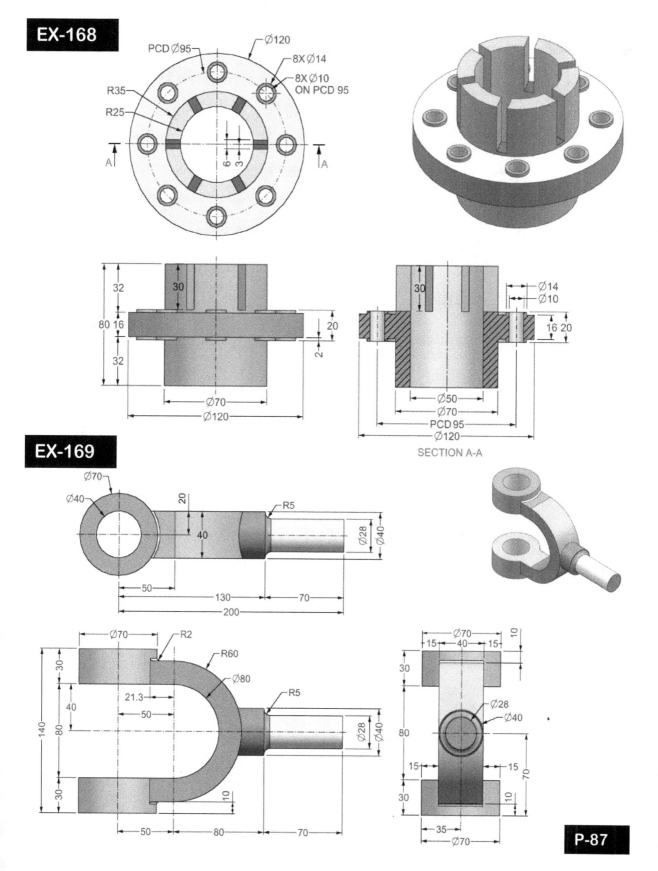

EX-168

PCD Ø95
Ø120
8X Ø14
8X Ø10
ON PCD 95
R35
R25

A   A

32
30
80 16
32
20
2

Ø70
Ø120

30
Ø14
Ø10
16 20

Ø50
Ø70
PCD 95
Ø120

SECTION A-A

EX-169

Ø70
Ø40
20
40
R5
Ø28
Ø40

50
130
70
200

Ø70
R2
R60
Ø80
R5

30
40
80
140
21.3
50
30
10
Ø28
Ø40

50
80
70

Ø70
15 40 15
10
30
80
15 15
70
Ø28
Ø40
30
10
35
Ø70

P-87

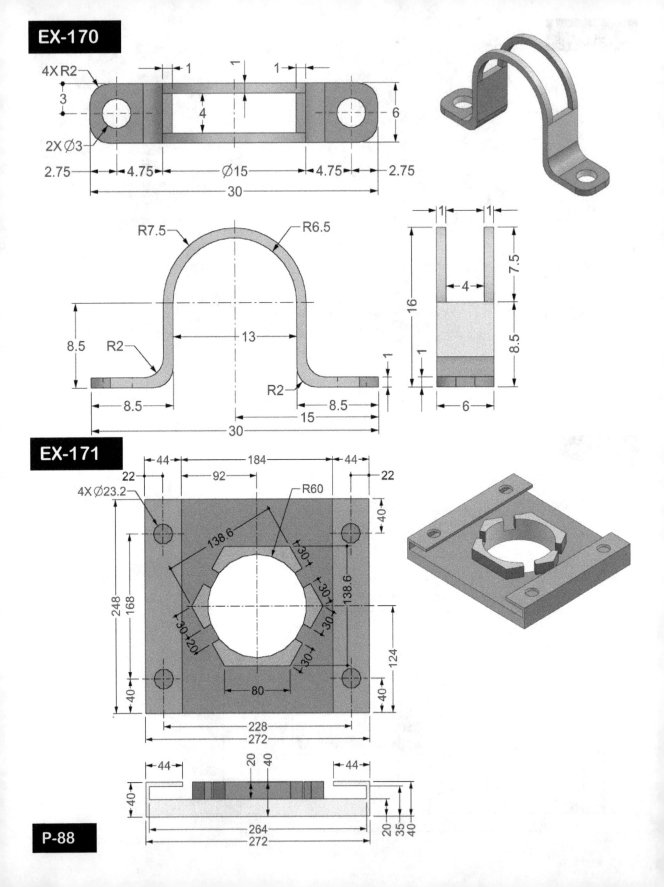

EX-170

4X R2
3
2X Ø3
2.75 — 4.75 — Ø15 — 4.75 — 2.75
30
1   1   1

4
6

R7.5   R6.5
R2
8.5
R2
8.5   8.5
15
30
13

1   1
7.5
4
16
8.5
1
1
6

EX-171

44 — 184 — 44
22   92   22
4X Ø23.2   R60
138.6   30
138.6
30
30   30
30
20
80
248   168   124
40   40
40   40
228
272

44   20   40   44
40   40
264   20   35   40
272

P-88

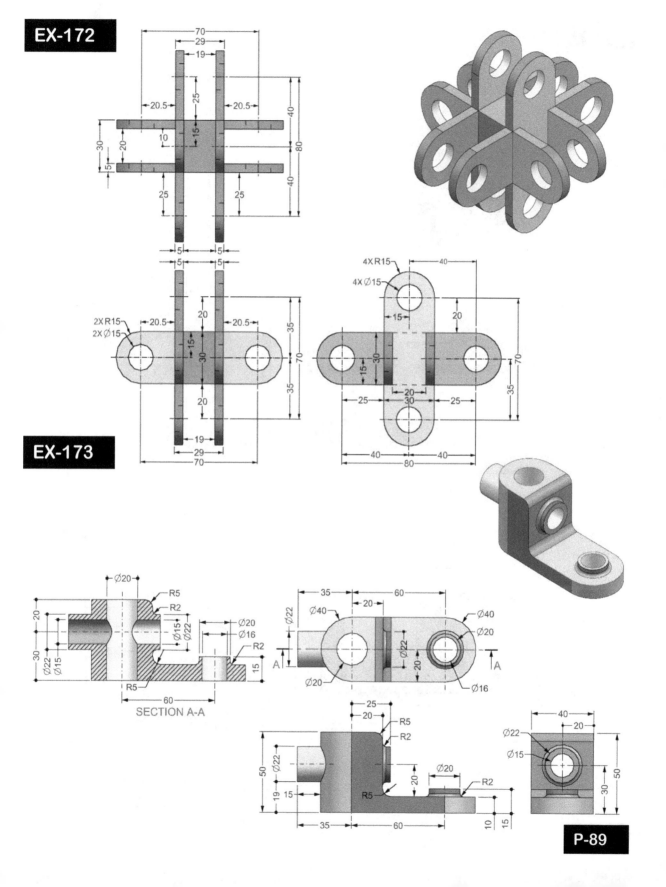

EX-172

EX-173

SECTION A-A

P-89

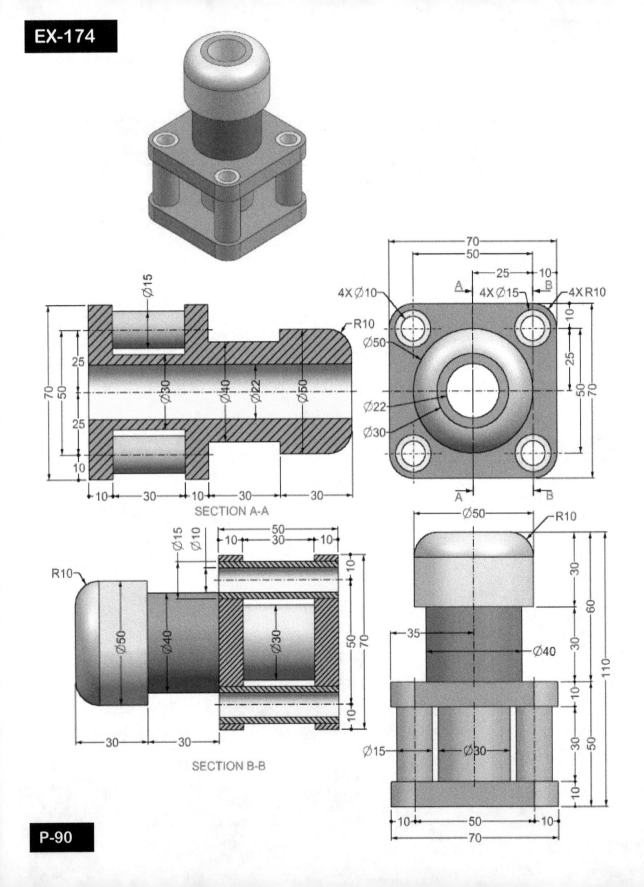

EX-174

SECTION A-A

SECTION B-B

P-90

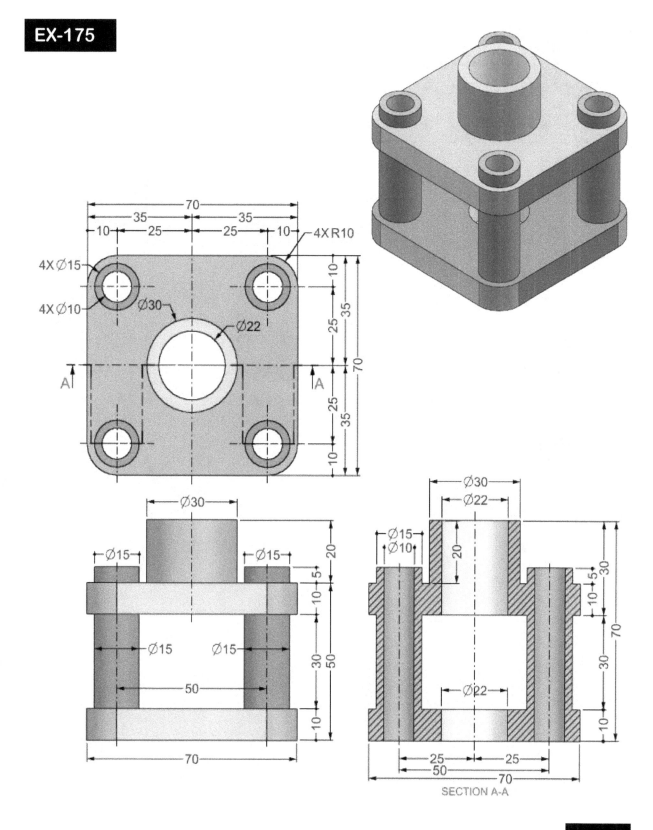

SECTION A-A

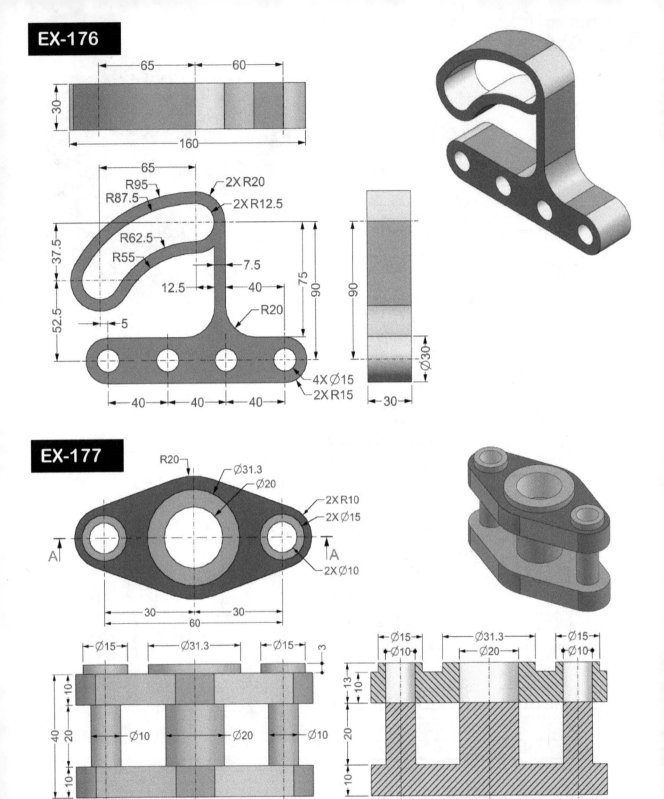

EX-176

65   60
30
160

65
R95
R87.5
2X R20
2X R12.5
R62.5
R55
37.5
7.5
12.5   40
5
52.5
R20
75
90
90
Ø30
4X Ø15
2X R15
40   40   40
30

EX-177

R20
Ø31.3
Ø20
2X R10
2X Ø15
A
A
2X Ø10
30   30
60

Ø15   Ø31.3   Ø15   3
10
40   20   Ø10   Ø20   Ø10
10
30   30
60

Ø15   Ø31.3   Ø15
Ø10   Ø20   Ø10
13
10
20
10
30   30
60
SECTION A-A

P-92

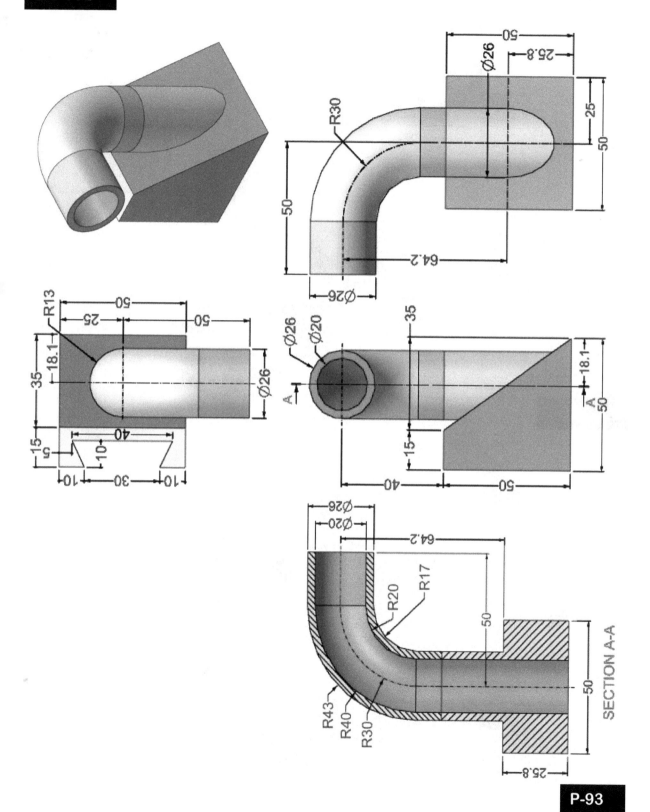

SECTION A-A

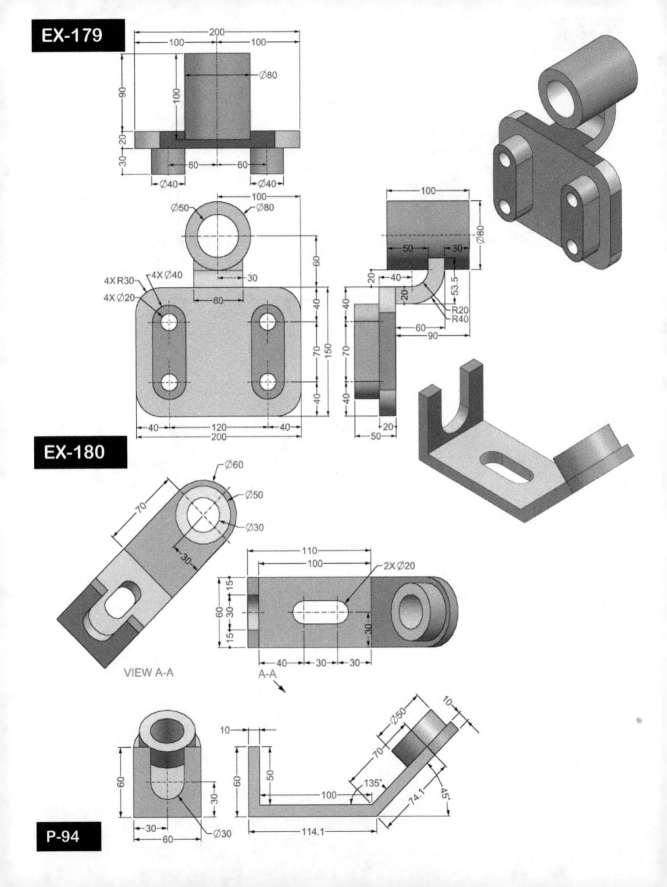

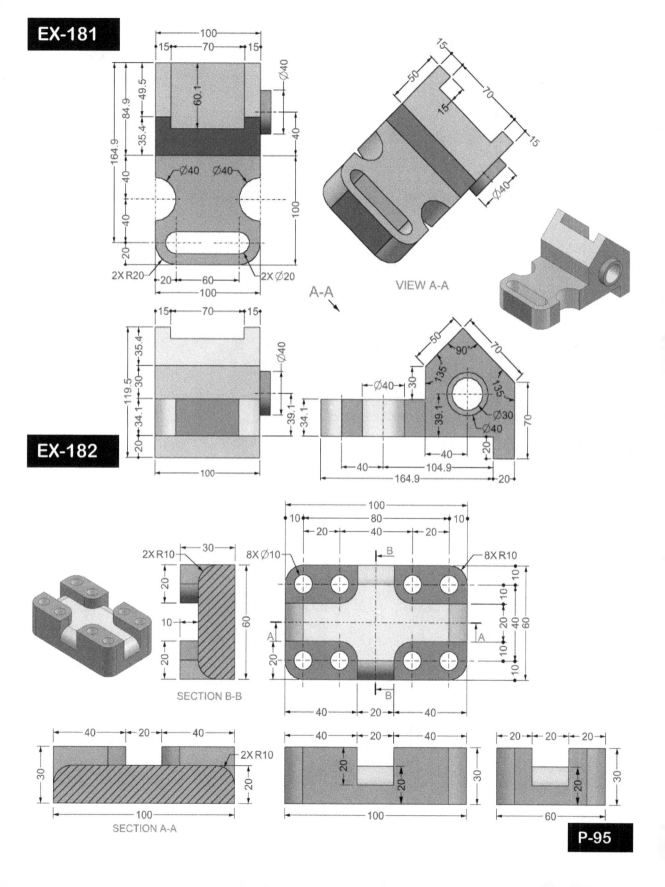

EX-181

100
15 70 15
Ø40
60.1
49.5
84.9
35.4
164.9
40
Ø40 Ø40
40
100
40
20
2X R20
2X Ø20
20 60
100

VIEW A-A

15
50
70
15
Ø40

A-A

EX-182

15 70 15
Ø40
35.4
30
119.5
34.1
39.1
20
100

50
90
Ø40
30
135
135
Ø30
39.1
Ø40
70
20
40
104.9
40
20
164.9

2X R10
30
8X Ø10
100
10 80 10
20 40 20
B
8X R10
20
10
10
20
40
60
10
10
A
A
20
60
B
40 20 40

SECTION B-B

40 20 40
2X R10
30
20
100

SECTION A-A

40 20 40
20
20
30
100

20 20 20
20
30
60

P-95

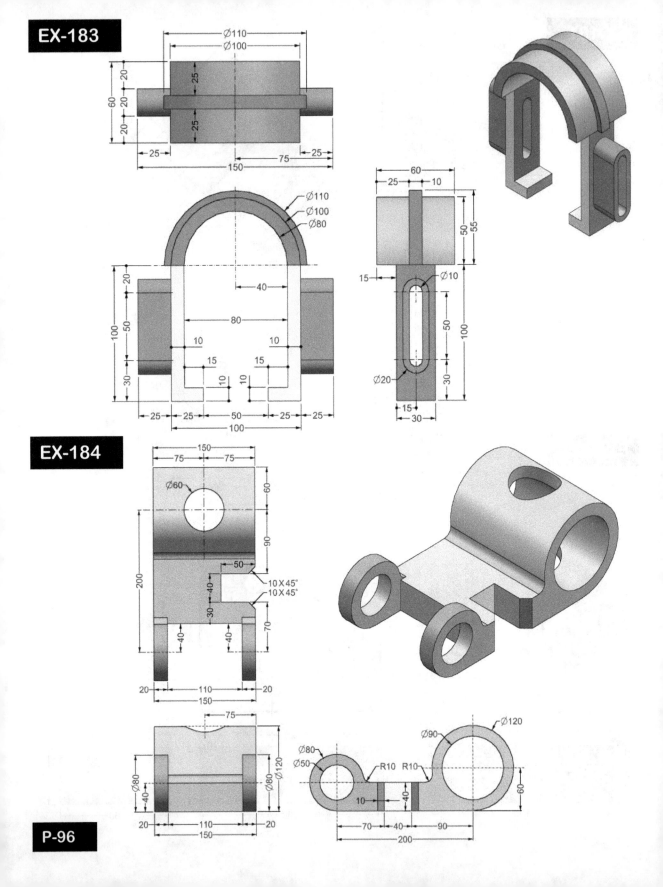

EX-183

Ø110
Ø100
20
20
60
20
25
25
25
75
25
150

Ø110
Ø100
Ø80
20
40
50
100
80
30
10
10
15
15
10
10
25
25
50
25
25
100

60
25
10
55
50
15
Ø10
50
100
30
Ø20
15
30

EX-184

150
75
75
Ø60
60
90
200
50
10 X 45°
40
10 X 45°
30
70
40
40
20
110
20
150

75
Ø80
Ø120
Ø80
40
20
110
20
150

Ø120
Ø90
Ø80
Ø50
R10 R10
10
40
60
70
40
90
200

P-96

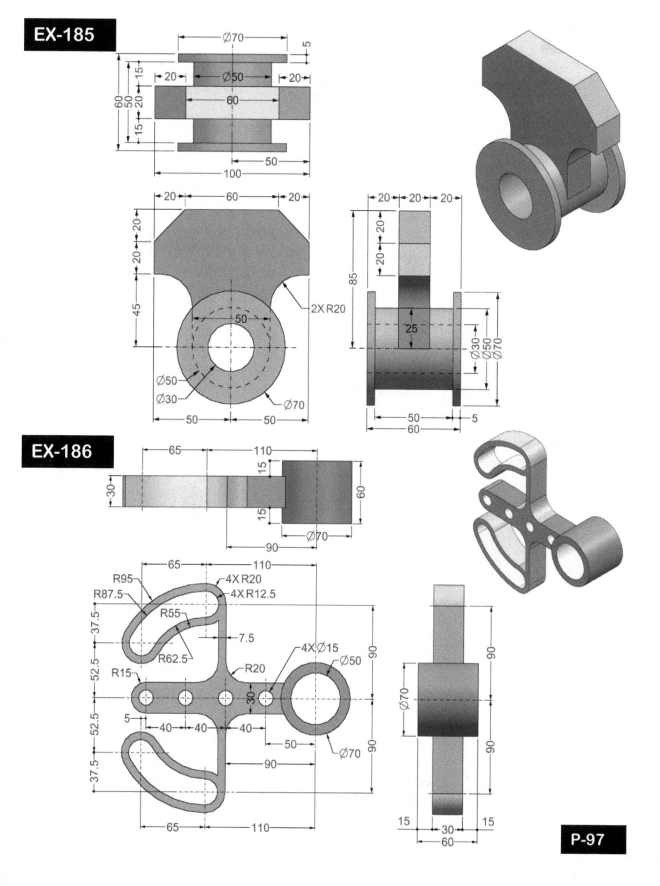

EX-185

EX-186

P-97

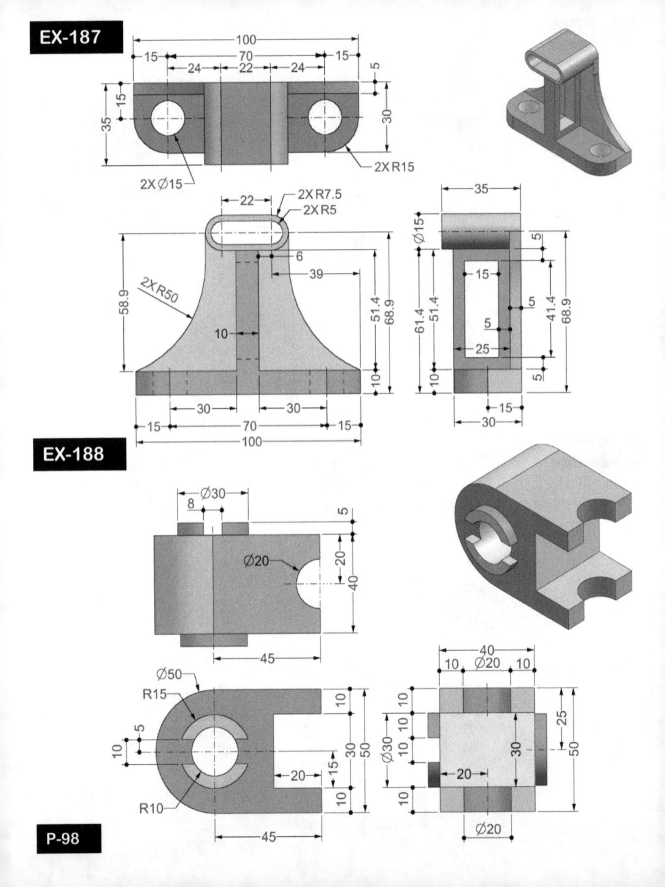

EX-187

100
15
70
15
24
22
24
5
35
15
30
2X R15
2X Ø15

2X R7.5
22
2X R5
6
58.9
39
2X R50
51.4
68.9
10
10
15
70
15
30
30
100

35
Ø15
5
15
5
61.4
51.4
41.4
68.9
5
25
10
5
15
30

EX-188

Ø30
8
5
Ø20
20
40
45

Ø50
R15
40
10
Ø20
10
5
10
30
50
20
15
Ø30
10
10
30
25
50
20
R10
10
45
Ø20

P-98

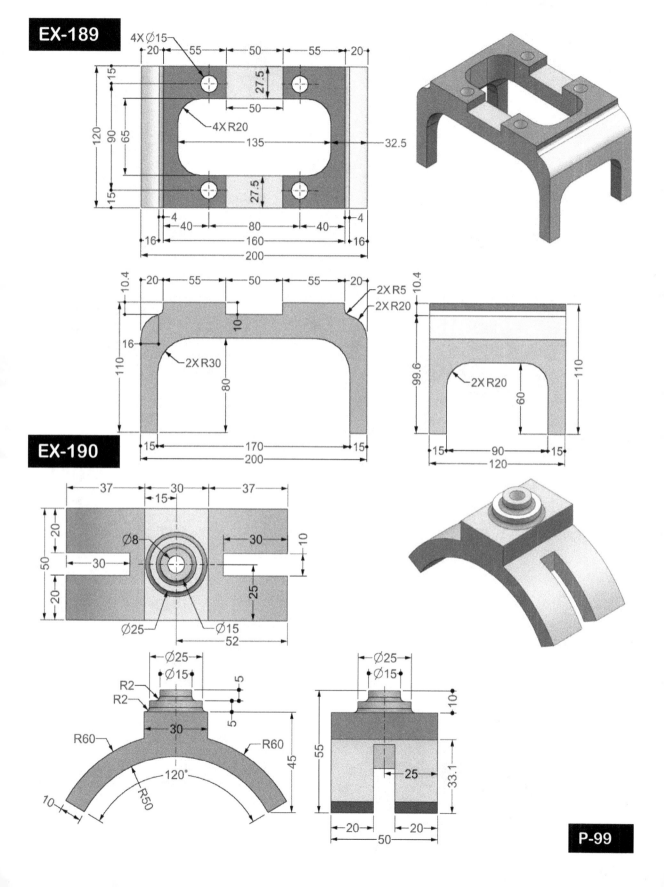

EX-189

4X Ø15

20 55 50 55 20
15
27.5
4X R20
50
120
90
65
135
32.5
15
27.5
4
40 80 40 4
16 160 16
200

10.4
20 55 50 55 20
2X R5
2X R20
10.4
10
16
110
2X R30
80
99.6
2X R20
110
60
EX-190
15 170 15
200
15 90 15
120

37 30 37
15
Ø8
30
10
50
20
30
25
20
Ø25 Ø15
52

Ø25
Ø15
R2
5
R2
5
R60
30
R60
R60
45
120°
R50
10
Ø25
Ø15
10
55
33.1
25
20 20
50

P-99

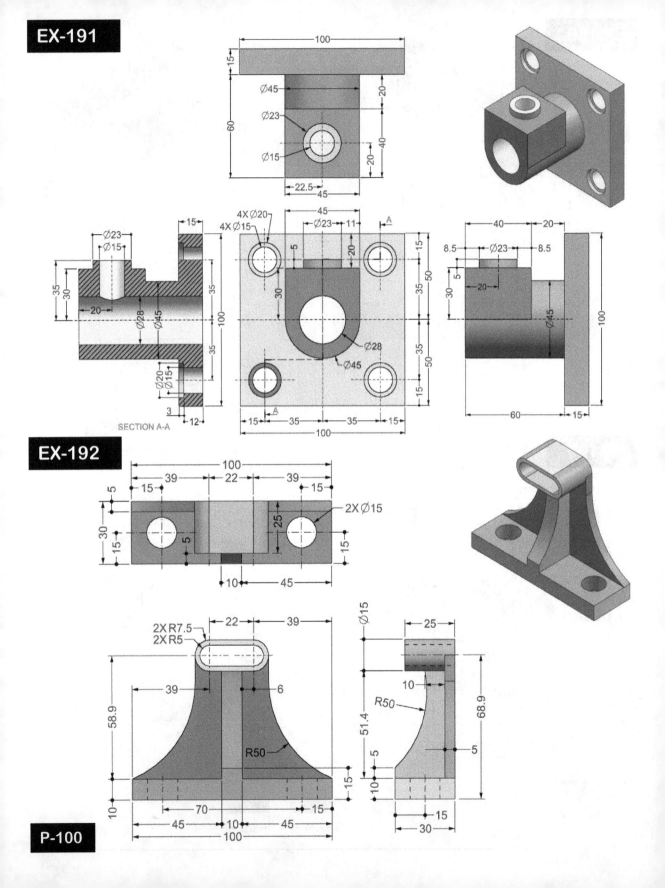

EX-191

SECTION A-A

EX-192

P-100

EX-193

SECTION A-A

40
12
10

10

R2

Ø20
Ø30

80
60

30

1 x 45°

10

Ø8
Ø14

A

2X Ø14
2X R10
2X Ø8
R20

Ø30

15

40

R20

30

60

30

10

Ø20

Ø30

55

Ø30
Ø23

R2
R2

15

Ø30

Ø14

40

12

10

55

40
Ø30

Ø14

20

R3.2

40

10
12

30   30
60

EX-194

150
110
20

4X Ø20
20

20

55

40

40

R5

15

130

30

15

60

40

Ø120

30

40   70   40
35

130°

ALL HOLES CHAMFER 2MM

2X Ø20
2X Ø50

Ø120

25°

R5

75

PCD Ø160
Ø100

80

R5

40   R5

40   70   40
35

20

60
30
15

80

30   40

20

R5

40
130

70

50

60

4X Ø20

20

20   110
150

BOTTOM VIEW

P-101

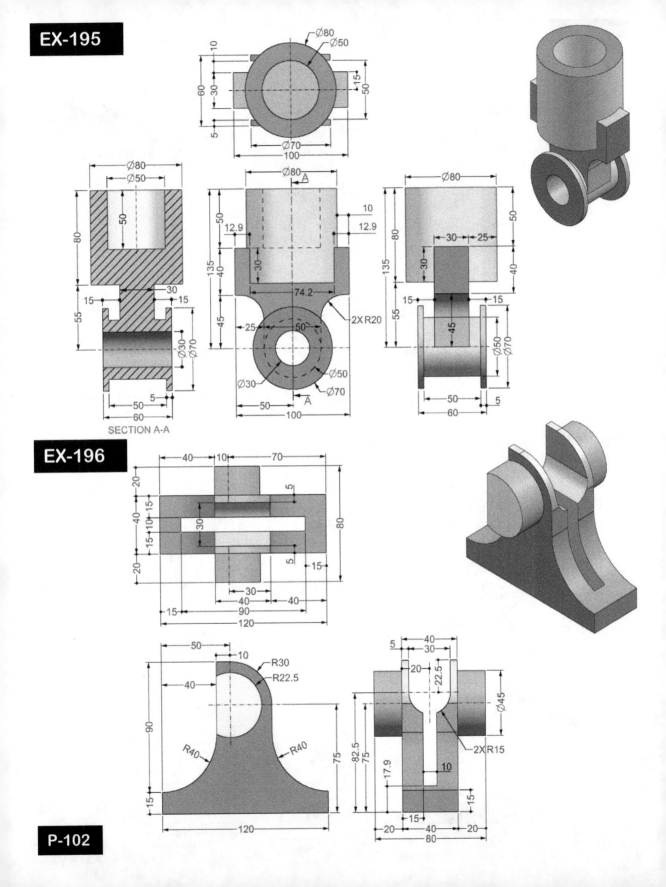

EX-195

Ø80
Ø50
10
60
30
15
50
5
Ø70
100

Ø80
Ø50
50
80
55
15 — 30 — 15
Ø30
Ø70
50 — 5
60
SECTION A-A

Ø80
A
50
135
40
30
12.9
74.2
2X R20
45
25 — 50
Ø30
Ø50
Ø70
50
100
A
10
12.9

Ø80
80
135
55
30 — 25
30
40
15 — 15
45
Ø50
Ø70
50 — 5
60

EX-196

40 — 10 — 70
20
40
15
10
30
5
80
15
20
5 — 15
30
40 — 40
15 — 90
120

50
10
R30
R22.5
90
40
R40
R40
75
15
120

5 — 40
30
20
22.5
Ø45
82.5
75
17.9
2X R15
10
15
15
20 — 40 — 20
80

P-102

EX-197

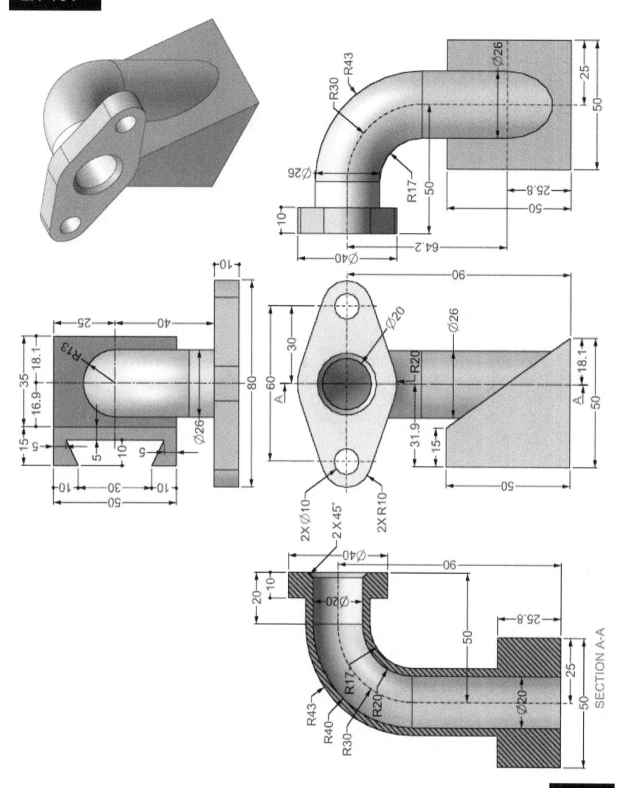

P-103

6X Ø15 THRU
ON PCD 90

Ø120

Ø50

Ø40

PCD Ø90

Ø20

8X Ø10 THRU
ON PCD 54

Ø30

Ø70

PCD Ø54

VIEW B-B

B-B

SECTION A-A

Ø120

Ø50

Ø40

15

10

Ø15

120

30

60°

80

Ø10

5

10

Ø20

Ø30 54

PCD 54

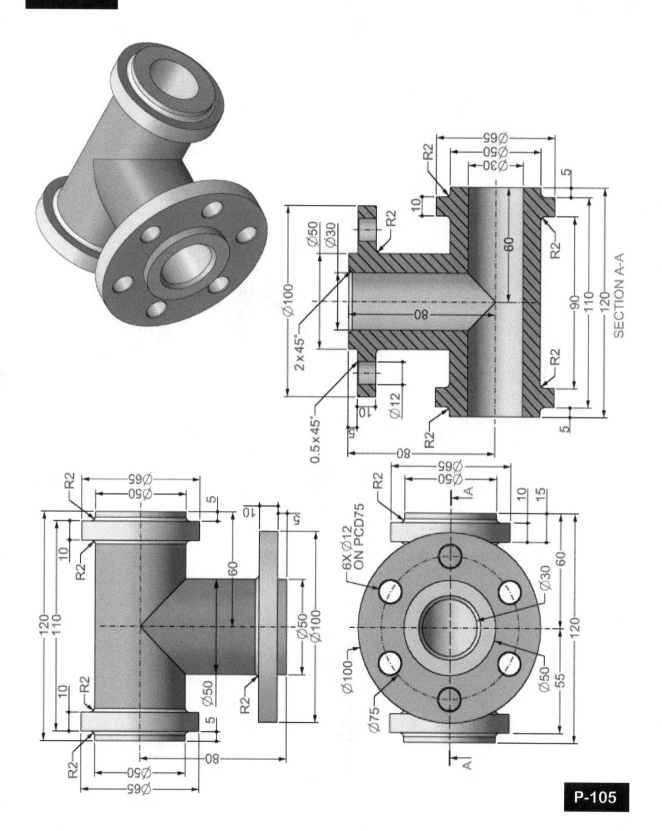

SECTION A-A

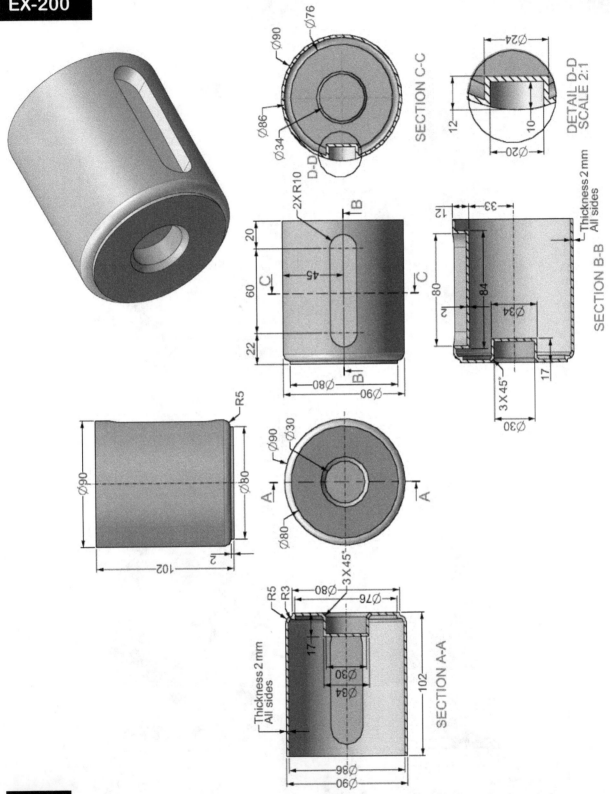

SECTION C-C

Ø76
Ø90
Ø86
Ø34
D-D

DETAIL D-D
SCALE 2:1
Ø24
12
10
Ø20

Thickness 2 mm
All sides

2XR10
B
20
C
45
60
22
C
B
Ø80
Ø90

SECTION B-B
12
33
80
8.4
Ø34
5
3 X 45°
17
Ø30

R5
Ø90
Ø80
102
2

Ø90
Ø30
A
A
Ø80

SECTION A-A
R5
R3
3 X 45°
Ø80
Ø76
17
Ø30
Ø84
Thickness 2 mm
All sides
102
Ø86
Ø90

Other useful books by CADIN360

1. 150 CAD Exercises

2. AutoCAD Exercises

3. CAD Exercises

4. 50+ SolidWorks Exercises

5. SolidWorks 200 Exercises

6. Autodesk Inventor Exercises

7. Catia Exercises

8. Siemens NX Exercises

www.ingramcontent.com/pod-product-compliance
Lightning Source LLC
Chambersburg PA
CBHW060447060326
40689CB00020B/4461